THE NATIONAL PURPOSE

The series on National Purpose appearing in *Life* magazine was produced under the supervision and with the help of the following members of the editorial staff:

Henry R. Luce
Editor-in-Chief

Hedley Donovan
Editorial Director

Edward K. Thompson
Managing Editor

Philip H. Wootton, Jr.
Assistant Managing Editor

Joseph Kastner
Copy Editor

Ralph Graves
Senior Editor

Oliver Allen
Edward Kern
Associate Editors

Terry Drucker
Jeanne Le Monnier
Assistant Editors

Betty Dunn
Diana Fetter
Grayce Horan
Giovanna Mancusi-Ungaro
Maya Pines
Louise Samuels
Ruth Silva
Martha Turner
Reporters

C. D. Jackson
Publisher

THE
NATIONAL
PURPOSE

by

JOHN K. JESSUP, ADLAI STEVENSON, ARCHIBALD
MAC LEISH, DAVID SARNOFF, BILLY GRAHAM,
JOHN W. GARDNER, CLINTON ROSSITER,
ALBERT WOHLSTETTER, JAMES RESTON,
and WALTER LIPPMANN

HOLT, RINEHART AND WINSTON   NEW YORK

Foreword

MORE THAN ANYTHING ELSE, THE PEOPLE OF AMERICA ARE asking for a clear sense of National Purpose.

In 1776 Thomas Jefferson wrote the Declaration of Independence. It said what the people of the colonies wanted and why. Without that Declaration, the United States of America might never have come into existence. For it took the words of the Declaration to unite a majority of the colonists in a clear purpose, involving a most difficult and painful struggle.

First the Declaration. Then Valley Forge. Then Victory. Then the Constitution. And today, from those foundations, the greatest nation in the world.

But what now shall Americans *do* with the greatness of their nation? And is it great enough? And is it great in the right way?

From all over the land, there is evidence that this is what Americans are worrying about. A group of citizens may begin by talking about the price of eggs or the merits of education but they end by asking each other: What are we trying to do, overall? Where are we trying to get? What is the National Purpose of the U.S.A.?

Some leaders say we should "sacrifice" more than we do; we should work harder, pay higher taxes. And one American answer is: Okay, but for what? By sacrificing and by working and by paying, what is it we expect to achieve?

Peace? Perhaps Peace is the No. 1 Purpose, but what

20071

kind of Peace—and, even, what do we do with Peace when we have it or if we get it?

Peace, of course, Peace in Freedom. But Freedom to do what? And be what?

To these questions of American purpose, *Life* recently asked ten thoughtful Americans to address themselves.

These articles, now brought together in this book, are offered as a summons, of some urgency, to a national debate.

—Henry R. Luce,
Editor-in-Chief
Life

Contents

I.   A Noble Framework for a Great Debate   1
     John K. Jessup

II.   "Extend our Vision . . . to All Mankind"   21
     Adlai Stevenson

III.   "We Have Purpose . . . We All Know It"   37
     Archibald MacLeish

IV.   "Turn the Cold War Tide in America's
     Favor"   49
     David Sarnoff

V.   "Men Must Be Changed Before a Nation Can"   61
     Billy Graham

VI.   Can We Count on More Dedicated People?   71
     John W. Gardner

VII.   We Must Show the Way to Enduring Peace   81
     Clinton Rossiter

VIII.   No Highway to High Purpose   95
     Albert Wohlstetter

IX.   Our History Suggests a Remedy   109
     James Reston

X.   National Purpose   125
     Walter Lippmann

     Appendix   135

THE NATIONAL PURPOSE

I

A Noble Framework for a Great Debate

John K. Jessup

"The critical weakness of our society is that for the time being our people do not have great purposes which they are united in wanting to achieve. The public mood of the country is defensive, to hold on and to conserve, not to push forward and to create. We talk about ourselves these days as if we were a completed society, one which has achieved its purposes, and has no further great business to transact. . . ."

So wrote Columnist Walter Lippmann a few months ago. It is a disturbing charge for three reasons. First, Lippmann is not alone in making it. The same complaint is heard, with varying emphasis, from many other critics and leaders of opinion, and also, according to a recent survey of

LIFE's correspondents, from many an average anonymous American as well. Some of them speak like Lippmann of our lost or mislaid national purpose or purposes; others use an older phrase, "the American dream." Thus William Faulkner: "What happened to the American dream? We dozed, and it abandoned us. And in that vacuum now there sound no longer the strong loud voices . . . speaking in mutual unification of one hope and will." As though he also felt something missing, the President himself has appointed a Commission on National Goals "to develop a broad outline of national objectives and programs for the next decade and longer." So much palpable concern, in quarters high and low, suggests that the vacuum of purpose may be a real one.

Second, the charge is disturbing because if it is true it is new. The U.S. has hitherto been a country associated with great purpose. If that purpose is now absent, we are not what we were. Is there not a connection between the rise of nations and great purposes, between the loss of purpose and their decline? A U.S. without a purpose, or no greater purpose than "Don't rock the boat," may well be a U.S. in decline.

Third, the world needs a purposeful America. Even if the U.S. could ever be a "completed society," to use Lippmann's phrase, the world is not. Mankind has much further "great business to transact"— if not with the active leadership of the U.S., then without it, and probably with the leadership of Communism.

It may be argued that Lippmann's charge, even if true, is irrelevant. Does the U.S. really need a self-conscious purpose in the world? Is not a democracy its own *raison d'être,* and survival the whole of its duty? Many feel that only individuals, not nations, are capable of high purposes; and that the proper role of the American nation is simply to provide the political framework in which each American citizen defines and conducts his own private "pursuit of happiness," nobly or ignobly, to suit himself. Yet this theory of a passive role for the nation has not satisfied the growing uneasiness. "Why are many Americans fearful that we have lost our sense of national purpose?" asks Adlai Stevenson. "Why is there a slackness about public problems and a wholesale retreat to the joys of private life?"

If America is in fact an elderly, *status quo* nation, it has had one of the briefest runs for its money in the history of great nations, and its early senescence will have belied more prophecies and grander promises than any nation ever made. During most of its brief history America has been bursting with confidence in its own unlimited destiny. A French visitor in the 1840's asked one of these confident spokesmen, Senator Lewis Cass of Michigan, "If such is the youth of the republic, what will be its old age?" Replied the senator, "Sir, it will have no old age." Cass's bold prophecy is already proved doubtful by the fact that so few Americans feel like repeating it today.

Thus there appears to be a real vacuum in the national will, or at least the widespread fear that such a vacuum exists. Does the U.S. lack a national purpose? Does it need a national purpose in the world? If so, what should that purpose be?

The present article is a résumé of what earlier generations have felt about the American national purpose, together with a few remarks on the new historical conditions that may have affected these beliefs. How far are the older beliefs relevant to the problems that face our country now, in this strange era of Communism, megaton weaponry, fractured empires, mushrooming sovereignties and continuing moral, social and technical revolution? The answers hinted at in this introduction are not offered as definitive. Fuller answers will be presented subsequently by leaders of opinion.

The motivating beliefs of a nation are to be sought in its deeds and illuminated by the words of its leaders, its spokesmen and its key documents. Deeds and words do not always match, but in America they have matched often enough to show a pattern to those who look for one. Thus when Roger Williams expounded the *principles* of religious liberty and democracy, his authority did not run beyond colonial Rhode Island; but the practical *experience* of mutual accommodation among the sects in other colonies eventually established religious liberty as part of the American political creed. Thus, too, township self-government and the common law, which helped to make the Constitution workable, were the slow deposit of English and colonial experience rather than the decree of towering prophets or statesmen. But on occasion sudden flashes of great documentary lightning have also illuminated our beliefs. The greatest of these was, of course, the Declaration of Independence on July 4, 1776.

The Declaration turned what had just a few months before been an Anglo-American family quarrel into a defiance of all tyranny everywhere. Colonial loyalty to the English crown, the dominant American sentiment of 1775, was transformed into national loyalty to the cause of political freedom for the human race.

Thomas Jefferson achieved his masterpiece not by taking an opinion poll, nor yet by sucking the words from his thumb. In writing the Declaration he borrowed some current political ideas from England, from Virginia, from Massachusetts, from Tom Paine and from other sources. He carefully listed the colonists' particular grievances against George III. But above all he related the cause of American independence to certain timeless beliefs about the nature of man, society and government.

Men are created with equal and inalienable rights—all men everywhere. The chief purpose of any government is to secure these rights, and its just power comes only from the consent of the governed. Although this news took decades to spread and has yet to penetrate everywhere, all other theories of government were doomed by this Declaration and the American independence that followed it. Tom Paine did not exaggerate: "Despotism felt a shock, and man began to contemplate redress." The Declaration went round the Western world, adding an important stimulus to the revolution in France, the independence of Latin America, the national movements in Germany, Italy, Greece and eastern Europe, and eventually to be reflected in the political reformation of England itself.

Small wonder, then, that in America the Declaration became the focus of that sense of special destiny and vocation which most vocal Americans had long associated with their country. Just as the Puritans had felt akin to the Israelites, chosen by God for a "holy experiment" in rule by conscience on new soil, so George Washington's generation felt themselves to be the vanguard of a new political dispensation. They were a watershed in human history, agents of what John Adams had called "a grand scheme and design in Providence for the illumination and emancipation of the slavish part of mankind all over the earth."

Added Adams: "The institutions now made in America will not wholly wear out for thousands of years. It is therefore of the last importance that they should be right." In this self-conscious spirit was our Constitution written. It was to be *the* test of the basic question whether men, as Alexander Hamilton put it, can achieve good government by "reflection and choice," or whether they must always be governed by "accident and force."

The Constitution was not a universal document in the same sense as the Declaration. It was a working document for Americans, not for Laplanders or Chinese. It has nevertheless proved an adequate political franchise for Americans while they subdued a continent, added 37 new states, fought seven wars and changed from an agricultural federal republic into an industrialized democratic nation. We have seen fit to amend the Constitution 22 times but not to change a word of the preamble, which is a summary statement of what the founders thought to be the true purposes of government—any government. Here are those purposes: "To form a more perfect Union, establish justice, insure domestic tranquillity, provide for the common defense, promote the general welfare, and secure the blessings of liberty."

These purposes, and the principle of strong but limited government under law which imbues it, have made the Constitution a focus of American patriotic reverence second only to the Declaration. It is a much stronger focus of loyalty, for example, than the American land, for all this land's purple majesty and beloved rocks and rills. An English visitor in 1837 remarked on the transient place-sense of this migratory people: "Give the American his institutions, and he cares little where you place him." Said Hawthorne, "We have so much country that we have really no country at all." The land has been an inestimable stimulus to effort and to wealth, but the system that enabled every man to take up his pursuit of wealth and happiness has been the most valued part of the whole. The American system has always been held to be far wider than American geography. As Walt Whitman said, repeating the idea in poem after poem, "O America, because you build for mankind I build for you."

• By Whitman's time the U.S., like its great poet, was taking pride in the title of "democracy," a word the Founding Fathers had not much liked. Our 19th Century legislation —from free schools and no-jail-for-debt to the Homestead Act, not to mention the emancipation of slaves—maintained an egalitarian bent. Its purpose and effect were to widen the suffrage and enlarge the opportunities of the average man. John Locke had made the amount of its emigration a test of whether a country is truly governed by consent or not. Waves of immigration, visibly assimilated, were evidence that America was the most consent-governed country in the world. As one not untypical immigrant wrote home: "Here a highway to honor, wealth and renown is open to all." Our national mission was to exemplify the success of free self-government, to let our democratic light so shine before men that they could see its good works and become democrats too. Many did, including most of Europe.

The first internationally recognized American historian, George Bancroft, saw American democracy as the highest revelation of God's purpose in history and the consummation of all previous civilizations. "In the fulness of time," he wrote, "a republic arose in the wilderness of America. Thousands of years had passed away before this child of the ages could be born . . . from her the human race drew hope." This viewpoint, which today sounds primitive or jingoistic, was as self-evident to many 19th Century Americans as the rights of man were to those of the 18th. Both were vindicated by continuing success. Indeed, the American experiment was succeeding in so many directions that the sense of national purpose, though no less intense, became somewhat diffuse. Patriotism became identified with practically every virtue except patience. Thus Emerson: "I wish to see America a benefactor such as no country ever was . . . the office of America is to liberate, to abolish king-craft, priestcraft, castle, monopoly, to pull down the gallows, to burn up the bloody statute-book, to take in the immigrant, to open the doors of the sea and the fields of the earth." In the swelling tide of immigration and expansion he also foresaw the advent of "a new race, a new religion, a new state, a new literature."

By the end of the 19th Century there were at least four great causes which America could be said to exemplify and which many Americans were eager to urge on the human race. These were:

1) *Democracy*. Bancroft called it "practical Christianity" and said: "The duty of America is to secure the culture and the happiness of the masses by their reliance on themselves." The people's voice was the voice of God, and of progress and of civilization as well.

2) *Individual liberty*. The wisdom of the Founding Fathers in making the free individual the cornerstone of our institutions was proved by his accomplishments. The individual was especially credited with our economic feats and therefore not begrudged his unequal rewards through the free enterprise system. He was the agent of that con-

quest of poverty which America had anticipated since colonial times.

3) *"Pluralism."* This became the scholar's word for our harmonious diversity of races, creeds and conditions. Scientist-Author E. E. Slosson was to define America as "the finest of all the fine arts, the art of getting along peaceably with all sorts and conditions of men." Our pluralistic laboratory proved the beneficence of the federal system, crowning our good with brotherhood from sea to shining sea. Since federalism had shown that it could govern and harmonize a continent, why not a world?

4) *Morality.* The universe is moral and "civilization depends on morality," said Emerson. Our system was assumed to be in closer touch than others with what Seward called "a higher law than the Constitution." The old Stephen Decatur formula, "our country, right or wrong," was offensive to intellectual patriots like Senator Carl Schurz, who amended it thus: "Our country . . . when right, to be kept right; when wrong, to be put right." Kept or set right by reliable methods, the vocal conscience of responsible citizens manifested itself through free institutions.

These four diverse national purposes could get somewhat out of alignment. Such was the case when Theodore Roosevelt came on the scene. Creative individualism had made it seem that America's dominant purpose—as it seems to many today—was merely to get rich. T. R., a great teacher as well as politician, used the White House as a pulpit to stir the national conscience to higher aims than the amassing of wealth. He preached the responsibility of the individual citizen, the social necessity of personal character, the central role of righteousness in democracy. He attacked that optimistic fatalism which assumed the coun-

try could always, in a contemporary's words, "slide down
hill into the valley of fulfillment" and warned that the
rights of men had to be freshly earned every day. He re-
asserted America's championship of popular rights. He
told us that "the history of America is now the central fea-
ture of the history of the world." He sought to put U.S.
foreign policy in the central position in that history, a position it was soon to occupy in fact.

American foreign policy before Teddy Roosevelt was
sometimes summarized as "the Monroe Doctrine and the
Golden Rule." Both were thoroughly consistent with
American beliefs. If the Monroe Doctrine seems too defensive today, it was for a century defiant of half the globe. It
aimed to keep European autocracy out of Latin America as
well as to allow the spread of democracy through our own
territorial expansion. It was not just the "manifest destiny"
of continental geography, but also democratic idealism
that carried our flag to California, Hawaii and the Philip-
pines. It was George Bancroft himself who, as acting Secretary of War, gave the order that sent U.S. troops into
Texas in 1846—just as young T. R., as Assistant Secretary
of the Navy, sent Commodore Dewey into Manila Bay in
1898.

Preoccupation with our own hemisphere did not always
blind us to the cause of freedom and democracy elsewhere.
National revolutionaries like Kossuth in Hungary, freely
admitting American inspiration, could also count on at
least unofficial American support. Commodore Perry in
opening Japan, John Hay in proclaiming the Open Door
against colonialism in China, Captain Mahan in his lec-
tures at the Naval War College—all were prophets of the

fact that American interests were becoming as global as the American cause.

In 1909 the Monroe Doctrine was re-analyzed by Herbert Croly, author of *The Promise of American Life,* which greatly influenced T. R.'s thinking. Now that Europe was democratized, Croly argued, Europe's interests and America's could no longer be considered "essentially incompatible," as some interpreters of the Doctrine had maintained. A time was coming when we would have to assume a wider and more active role. George Washington, in his Farewell Address, had enjoined us to avoid foreign entanglements and "give to mankind the magnanimous and too novel example of a people always guided by an exalted justice and benevolence." These words, said Croly, had been more honored in the letter than in the spirit. The time was coming when we should *seek* allies in order to build democracy into "a world system." In such a system, peace would inevitably depend on "the righteous use of superior force," and America's force would be needed on that righteous side.

Croly's contemporary patriots, however, were happier setting a no-longer-so-novel example than leading a magnanimous crusade. They responded more to the idea of a happy American destiny than to a clear American purpose. To Woodrow Wilson fell the sad task of proving the unreality of this distinction and of testing the American devotion to righteousness in a great European war. His war message of April 2, 1917 linked our destiny with that of democracy all over the world:

"The world must be made safe for democracy. Its peace must be planted upon the tested foundations of political liberty. . . . Civilization itself seeming to be in the balance. But the right is more precious than peace, and we shall

fight for the things which we have always carried nearest
our hearts—for democracy, for the right of those who submit to authority to have a voice in their own governments,
for the rights and liberties of small nations, for a universal
dominion of right by such a concert of free peoples as shall
bring peace and safety to all nations and make the world
itself at last free. . . . America is privileged to spend her
blood and her might for the principles that gave her
birth. . . ."

The "concert of free peoples" eventually became the
Wilson-inspired League of Nations. The League failed for
various reasons, but one of them was surely the failure of
follow-through in America's political will. Another and
even greater war, another and even more "pluralistic"
league called the United Nations, and the Wilson-era failure has at least been patched up. Said Franklin Roosevelt
in 1945: "We have learned that we cannot live alone, at
peace; that our own wellbeing is dependent upon the well-
being of other nations far away."

The Preamble and the stated Purposes of the U.N. contain many statements in which Americans can take pride,
since they could never have been written had not America
long preached and exemplified them—most notably the
declaration of "equal rights of men and women and of
nations large and small." Yet this declaration is made hypo-
critical by the nature of the U.N.'s membership, which
includes Communist states and thus severs the cause of
peace from its anchor in freedom and principle. The word
"righteousness," which to Wilson as to T.R. was synony-
mous with the higher patriotism, was not popularized by
F.D.R., is not used in the U.N. charter and is seldom heard
in its debates.

Wilson's war message was in many ways the last great documentary link between modern America and "the principles that gave her birth." Its echoes of the Declaration of Independence are not mere rhetoric. Those echoes had been enriched for Wilson's generation by the memory of our most profound national experience, the Civil War, and our greatest spokesman of national purpose, Abraham Lincoln.

Lincoln's first show of "stubborn grandeur," said Carl Sandburg, was in the passionate seriousness with which he took the words of the Declaration. To him it was a charter of political truth for "augmenting the happiness and value of life to all people of all colors everywhere." Because slavery was incompatible with the Declaration, the Declaration was the real issue of the Civil War. But this issue had been so long evaded and compromised that Lincoln could exploit it only within the larger cause of saving the Union. Thus political and military necessities robbed the words of his Emancipation Proclamation of great documentary lightning, but the deed was as "fundamental and astounding" as anything he said. Forced into the Constitution by war, by conscience and by the Declaration, the Proclamation was what Whitman called "by far the greatest revolutionary step in the history of the U.S."

Lincoln's greatness was more than verbal. It lay in the resolution with which he preserved the idea of union through our most tragic crisis. Such resolution could be sustained only by faith in "the proposition that all men are created equal." The national purpose that Lincoln stated for the union was that free government of the people, by the people and for the people should not perish from the earth.

Since Lincoln's time government by the people has been broadened step by step and deepened here and abroad with a cumulative effect scarcely less revolutionary than the Emancipation Proclamation itself. The abstraction for which Lincoln fought is now operative in more than half the world. Scores of new nations have been born since World War I because of the conviction that men should govern themselves, and the 1960 crop will be at least a half dozen more in Africa alone. Yet the popularity of Lincoln's abstraction has not made democracy any safer. On the contrary, some of the nations for whose freedom we fought under Wilson and Franklin Roosevelt, notably in eastern Europe and the Far East, have long since succumbed to ancient tyranny in its newest and most insidious guise, Communism. In all countries the new tyranny, like the old, is still abetted by ignorance and poverty, and in the poorer ones by a widespread belief that freedom and morality are luxuries—"first the grub, then the morals." Meanwhile in America, suffused in real luxuries, freedom and morality are taken for granted as casually as bread.

This does not mean that the U.S. has altogether forsaken its traditional purposes in foreign affairs. They have guided our reactions to many new and puzzling challenges, such generally creditable reactions as the Marshall Plan, the North Atlantic treaty, the defense of Korea, the upholding of the U.N. in the Suez and other crises, the spending of billions for alliances and aid. At vast expense but with fair success, the U.S. has contained Communism since 1949. We have defended the chance of many nations to choose freedom and establish self-government, from Guatemala to Vietnam.

But at other times and places we have failed to defend

this right. From Hungary in 1956 the appeal to American principles for American help was so direct and unmistakable that many Americans, in our government's blank failure to respond, thought they heard the snapping of a great cord to the most precious part of our past. To others this sound was muffled by the very scope and complexity of the challenge, for tyranny is only one of the conditions of human life that wears a new, confusing and very non-18th Century mask.

The whole order of organized power has changed. The once worthy title of "nation" may now denote either a monster or a pygmy state. Both weaponry and economics have made nonsense of long established boundaries between nations. Strange new alignments seem to be forming, one perhaps being an alignment of races. The scientific and technical revolution, which has already overthrown the social structure of some very old nations, may have overnight changes in store for many others, either from within their own laboratories or from some point in outer space. As for what Communism has done to international politics, in the words of a recent Rockefeller Brothers Fund report, "The chessboard itself may be said to have disappeared."

Nation states may no longer be the most meaningful integers of creative political thought. No existing state is or can be safe for democracy or freedom. Whatever may be hoped or feared from regional or racial alignments, any lasting political purpose must take the whole great globe for its arena. Nor is it just the Ghanaian, or the American, whose chance at happiness is threatened by technology. Human nature itself is threatened by dehumanization. A great political purpose today must have something to say about human nature, how to keep it as human and as rational as may be.

Such are the fantastic new conditions in which our old beliefs must find a home, a grave or a toehold. How can we best adapt our beliefs to the conditions? What purposes may rightfully be considered today?

Survival. Sensible patriots have proposed that our true cause today is sheer national survival. They say that this is important enough, and doubtful enough, to engage our full attention. Biology tells us that survival is a primary concern. Yet if survival by military means is meant, modern weapons are two-edged. Our present strategy of nuclear deterrence, if ever tested, could so reduce our population that its survivors, the bearers of our beliefs about liberty and self-government, might prefer to live elsewhere. On the other hand, since America is now the world's chief home and hope of freedom, a refusal to defend it could demoralize the cause of freedom for a thousand years. From this dilemma the only escape is to perceive that survival alone is not an adequate goal.

What is, then? No single goal, perhaps. A great power's foreign policy cannot be reduced to a phrase. The Council on Foreign Relations, analyzing our "Basic Aims" for the Senate Foreign Relations Committee, made a multiple recommendation: that while maintaining our negative policy of resisting and containing Communism, we must at the same time do much more to anticipate "the world's other problems," and try to link the non-Communist nations more closely through more and better institutions of law and order, security, economic development, freedom and peace. A large order!—but not necessarily an inspiring one. Although the U.S. has virtually unlimited responsibilities, can it respond to all alarms everywhere in the free world at once?

Self-government. The one principle that Americans have preached most consistently since their own founding is that men can govern themselves in freedom under law, and that all of them deserve a chance to try. Perhaps this simple message is too 18th Century for the world's needs today, or America's complex relation to it. But the millions who have not yet had their chance seldom say so. Self-government is clearly a central purpose for many peoples of the world.

Moral Law. Democracy, though we have treasured it, is not the highest value known to man. Indeed, it is only because enough Americans have had still higher allegiances that we have made democracy work.

America's public love affair with righteousness, for example, was not confined to the speeches of T.R. It began with the Mayflower Compact, whose ultimate purpose was the quest of God's truth. The same quest underlay our insistence on religious freedom, and the assumption of a moral order in the universe underlies much of our constitutional law. Said John Marshall, the great interpreter of the Constitution: "There are principles of abstract justice which the Creator of all things has impressed on the mind of his creature man, and which are admitted to regulate in great degree the right of civilized nations." Our very right to self-government is derived from "the Laws of Nature and of Nature's God," and to its harmony with these laws democracy owes its moral sanction.

If this moral order of the universe exists in fact—if there is such a thing as the Natural Law in which our Founding Fathers trusted—then it is surely the highest of man's political purposes to contrive his human institutions in conformity with this order, while realizing that all human institutions are subject to constant change. No more challenging task faces American leaders and intellectuals, if they believe in natural law, than to find its mundane applications in this revolutionary age. Certainly there resides in every human breast a natural instinct for justice, which experience has refined into the world's systems of law. A world that needs peace, which is the work of justice, needs clearer codifications of its sense of justice—*i.e.,* more and better national and international law.

But those of us who make World Law our national purpose must be sure the positive laws that we champion enjoy maximum consent. For example, by throwing its economic weight around, the U.S. can do much to promote free enterprise and freer trade in the non-Communist world. But it could do this better with less friction if Americans should produce a new definition of the right to property, which John Locke and our Founding Fathers considered basic to liberty. Such a definition would have to appear in harmony with natural justice to farmers and workers as well as to businessmen in all industrialized societies.

Private Purposes. Many Americans will approve the above-mentioned purposes and still deny that they should be avowed by the nation or its government. A consensus of private purposes can give shape and direction to our national life without getting into formal policy at all. Yet "in the fatness of these pursy times" our private purposes do not add up to anything so firm. As one Air Force lieutenant wrote to TIME, "What America stands for is making money, and as the society approaches affluence, its members are left to stew in their own ennui."

As monarchies were said to live by honor, so republics live by virtue. Yet republics have no public means of supplying a lack of virtue in the sovereign people. The public educational system can set and inculcate standards of the mind, and with this aim the Rockefeller Brothers Fund proposed to raise these standards, calling its report on our schools *The Pursuit of Excellence.* Even the citizen who thinks that virtue is old-fashioned, or that it is none of the state's business, can perhaps subscribe to excellence as a public purpose, and in a context of intellectual excellence, moral excellence (which must always be an individual purpose and achievement) may have a better chance. As T.R. used to say, a patriot will make the most of himself. If enough do, so will the nation.

II

"Extend our Vision . . .
to All Mankind"

ADLAI STEVENSON

IT IS NOT TOO DIFFICULT, I THINK, TO STATE THE CLASSIC
goals and purposes of American society. We probably cannot improve on the definition offered by our Founding
Fathers: "to form a more perfect union, establish justice,
insure domestic tranquillity, provide for the common de-
fence, promote the general welfare and secure the blessings
of liberty." Add Tom Paine's words—"My country is the
world; my countrymen are all mankind"—to give our goals
universal application, and we have distilled the essence
out of all the rhetoric about the freedom and democratic
self-government for which we proudly stand.

But the difficulty is that aims in the abstract mean little.
Communist double-talk—with "peace" meaning "cold

war," "people's democracy" meaning dictatorship, and "liberation" meaning domination—is reminder enough that what gives depth and direction to national purpose is not phrase-making but the way a society actually behaves, its manner of realizing its aims, where it lays up its treasure, the dream it carries closest to its heart. A society, in short, is measured by what it does, and no grandiloquent rhetoric, no Fourth of July oratory, will make its purposes great if in fact they are small, or change them into a moving element in the world's passionate dialogue of destiny if they are meager and private and unconcerned.

We have therefore to look at our noble purpose of freedom—and surely no one would deny that it is the organizing principle of American life—in terms of the concrete, practical content which Americans give to the concept. As one might expect in a free society, we encounter at once that freedom itself has many meanings and has implied different things to different people at different times in our national life. In fact one can observe something of a rhythm in the nation's mood, a swing from one definition of freedom almost to its opposite, recurring regularly throughout the almost 200 years of our independent history.

The first mood reflects the *private* aspect of freedom— the right of men to choose their own ideas and pursuits, to be free from the arbitrary interventions of government, to "do what they like with their own." Many early immigrants were especially aware of this freedom in the economic sphere. They escaped the arbitrary restraints of governments in Europe and came to set their money and their wits to work in the new climate of enterprise. This sense of the link between "freedom" and private business has indeed been so strong that at some periods they have virtually been equated, as when Calvin Coolidge thus defined the American purpose: "The business of America is—business."

But equally freedom has had its *public* aspect as the organizing principle of a new kind of society. In the Declaration of Independence, the basic charter of the modern world, the picture is of a great civic order in which governments, deriving their authority from the consent of the governed, help to secure the inalienable pre-conditions of the good life—equality before the law and in human respect, life, liberty and, most precious yet intangible of rights, the pursuit of happiness. This positive vision of society in which public authority plays its essential part in bettering the lot of all citizens is as inherent as freedom itself in the vision of our founders and philosophers.

There is no inevitable contradiction between these public and private aspects of American society. Indeed, they are the essential poles of energy in a vigorous social order. Without individual decision and inventiveness, without widely dispersed centers of authority and responsibility, the social order grows rigid and centralized. Spontaneity withers before the killing frost of public conformity. Individual citizens with all their varied relationships—as parents, neighbors, churchgoers, workers, businessmen—are reduced to the single loyalties of party and state. In this century we are not likely to underestimate that risk. We have seen free societies destroyed in this way by totalitarians of both the right and the left.

Yet the pursuit of private interest and well-being does not, as the 18th Century sometimes naively believed, automatically add up to the well-being of all. We cannot, like the poet Pope, believe that some divine ordering has bidden "self love and social be the same." They are not. The strong pursuit of *my* interest can override the vital interests of others, if nature, health, energy and property have weighted the odds in my favor. Social evils pile up when little beyond unchecked private interest determines the pattern of society.

At best, the result is a "lobby" or "pressure group" state in which each organized group jostles for its own interests, at the expense of the weak, the isolated or the unorganized. France under the Third and Fourth Republic had something of this quality—a republic of interests and buddies, not of principles and patriots.

At worst, the power and influence of the few can violate the fundamental rights and decencies of the many—as in the long survival of human slavery, and in the long resistance of industry to child labor laws and minimum wages. And in our own prosperous days, a new possibility has arisen—that the many can smugly overlook the squalor and misery of the few and tolerate, in the midst of unparalleled plenty, ugly slums, rural destitution and second class citizenship.

It is the often mediocre and sometimes intolerable consequences of unchecked private interest that have led to the reassertion, at regular intervals in American history, of the primacy of public good. The concept of government as an evil to be reduced to the smallest possible proportions gives place to the idea—in keeping with the vision of the Founders—of government as a positive instrument designed to secure the well-being of all America's citizens. Sometimes, the swing occurs because evil has become so obtrusive that only vigorous public action can check it in time.

The conviction that the spread of slavery endangered the Union itself helped to precipitate the Civil War. The demoralization of the entire economy after 1929 led to the experiments and reforms of Roosevelt's New Deal.

Sometimes the swing seems to occur in response to subtler promptings. Early in this century, for instance, under Theodore Roosevelt and Woodrow Wilson, it was not imminent social collapse but disgust at the smash and grab materialism which was devouring America that aroused people once more to demand the restatement of America's public purposes and a new vision of the common good.

Whatever the reasons for America's recurrent swing in emphasis from private interest to public responsibility, it has always had a significant *external* consequence. It has aroused both in America and in the world at large the sense, eloquently expressed by our greatest statesmen, that the American experiment has significance far beyond its own frontiers and is in some measure a portent for all mankind. The feeling of a new dawn for all humanity echoes through the great utterances and documents which are the foundation of the United States of America. In his time, the Declaration of Independence meant for Lincoln that victory in the war against slavery and disunion was indispensable to the survival of free government everywhere, and was the promise, too, that ultimately humanity's age-old burdens would be lifted from the shoulders of all mankind.

Still later Woodrow Wilson spoke of "making the world safe for democracy" and sought in his idea of the League of Nations to work out a pattern of free association under law for the emergent society of man. And from the reforming ferment of the New Deal followed the Atlantic Charter, American initiative in forming the United Nations, and the derivative new experiments in economic assistance, which, launched with the Marshall Plan, have opened a new phase in the effort to build a genuinely humane order in our neighborhood, the world.

*   *   *

Today I don't suppose anyone will deny that mankind is in acute need of a convincing working model of a free society. Never in human history has there been an epoch of such profound and sudden social upheaval on so universal a scale. Never has the working model of tyranny made such claims for its own effectiveness; never has monolithic discipline attacked so savagely what it calls the pretensions of the free way of life. The whole of human society has become plastic and malleable in the flames of social revolution. Human energies everywhere are seeking to run into new molds and the Communists universally claim that theirs alone is the truly effective system.

Thus there has never been a time when the *public* aspect of American liberty as the organizing principle of a great social order has needed to be more studied and stressed.

But what do we find? Never before in my lifetime—not even in the days of Harding and Coolidge—has the mystique of privacy seemed to me so pervasive. The face which we present to the world—especially through our mass circulation media—is the face of the individual or the family as a high consumption unit with minimal social links or responsibilities—father happily drinking his favorite beer, mother dreamily fondling soft garments

newly rinsed in a marvel detergent, the children gaily calling from the new barbecue pit for a famous sauce for their
steak. And, of course, a sleek new car is in the background.

No doubt many of the world's peoples want and mean
to get a lot more of this. But it is not *all* they want, and
they have to look hard to find the balancing picture of
America's wider purposes and to learn that high private
consumption is not our ultimate aim of life, nor our
answer to all man's evils and disorders in a time of breath-
taking social change. I think of the Psalmist's words: "And
He gave them that which they lusted after, and sent lean-
ness withal into their soul." High consumption is not
spiritual growth. Nor is it the same as cultural growth.
Gerald Johnson has used the phrase "America's high
standard of low living." And all these good "things" do
not solve the problems of urban decay and congestion.
Behind the shining child in the advertisement lurks the
juvenile delinquent in the run-down slum. Nor does high
consumption solve the sprawl of subdivisions which is
gradually depriving us of either civilized urban living or
uncluttered rural space. It does not guarantee America's
children the teachers or the schools which should be their
birthright. It does nothing to end the shame of racial dis-
crimination. It does not counter the exorbitant cost of
health, nor conserve the nation's precious reserves of land
and water and wilderness.

The contrast between private opulence and public
squalor on most of our panorama is now too obvious to be
denied. Yet we still spend per capita almost as much on
advertising to multiply the private wants of our people as
we do in educating them to seek a fuller, wiser and more
satisfying civic existence. Nor is this imbalance simply a

matter of drift and the unmeant consequence of our fabulous new opportunities for wealth creation. It is in real measure the result of considered and deliberate government policy. Except for defense American public expenditure today is proportionately lower than it was in 1939. Moreover, it is lower than current levels in West Germany, Belgium, Britain or Sweden—to take a European cross-section of capitalist economies. And while we raise a cheer at the comparison, let us also remember that it means a relative decline in support for such basic needs as schooling, research, health, small income housing, urban renewal, and all forms of public services—local, state and federal—at a time when there has been steadily more income to spend on every private want, or unwant.

With the supermarket as our temple and the singing commercial as our litany, are we likely to fire the world with an irresistible vision of America's exalted purposes and inspiring way of life?

Even where public spending has been high—for defense and economic aid—our performance has been more defensive than indicative of freedom's positive purposes. We have stressed so much our aim of stopping Communism for our own security that self-interest has often contaminated our generous aid programs. And even in the vital field of military security the Administration's concern for the citizen as a private consumer rather than as a mature responsible American who will accept the unpleasant facts about his security, leaves one with the lurking doubt that budgetary considerations, rather than the stark needs of strategy, are determining our defense effort.

In short, at a time of universal social upheaval and challenge, our vision of our own society seems to be of limited

social significance. In the most public and civic of epochs—
when the fate of nations and civilizations is the common
theme of the world's discourse—we have drawn back and
taken refuge in the joys of privacy. An air of disengagement and disinterest hangs over the most powerful and
affluent society the world has ever known. Neither the
turbulence of the world abroad nor the fatness and flat-
ness of the world at home are moving us to more vital
effort. We seem becalmed in a season of storm, drifting in
a century of mighty dreams and great achievements. As
an American I am disturbed.

*　　*　　*

John Adams said that at the time of the American Revolution never more than a third of the colonists really
wanted independence. And probably even less cared to
make the exertion independence demanded. A third were
loyal to the King, and the rest were inert and uncommitted.

So the condition of our public discourse and individual
freedom today is not one for despair or even much dis-
couragement. And it is arguable that after the shocks and
rigors of the 1930s and '40s, we as a nation needed a period
of relaxation—though I would note that the Russians and
the Chinese after far greater shocks have had no opportunity for a cozy nap. Now, however, we have had our rest,
and I sense the stirring of a new vitality, possibly the beginning of that traditional swing of the political pendulum
away from private pursuits to a concern for the nation's
broader purposes, which has always provided the strong
oscillating balance in our American experiment of
freedom.

I am persuaded that the leaders and the parties which

now speak clearly to the Americans of their social responsibilities, as well as their private wants, will command a
more attentive hearing. I believe the old idea of America
and its government as a positive instrument for the common weal is being restored once again after all the cheap
sarcasm about "bureaucracy" and "creeping socialism."
And if a change of mood and attitude toward our public
needs and institutions is in fact on the way, I do not think
there can be much question about the fields in which the
new sense of responsibility must quickly go to work.

At home we must ask ourselves again what *quality* of
life we want, both public and private, not simply as consumers and producers but as citizens of this great republic.
Education and the arts is the starting point, for it is only
here that the citizens of tomorrow can learn to demand and
live a fuller life. A respect for excellence and a sense of
discipline in the attainment of knowledge are virtues not
just because the Russians pioneered the space age and
photographed the dark side of the moon, but because the
new society that technology is building demands a grasp
and competence among the mass of citizens undreamed of
in earlier civilizations.

By education and the arts we mean something more than
better school buildings, higher teachers' salaries, and more
scholarships for the intelligent. We mean a reorientation
of our ideals and tastes, the strenuous stretching of mental
and artistic talent, the exaltation of excellence above social
approval, and of mental achievement above quick material
success. We mean, in short, new standards of respect and
reward for intellect and culture. And we mean more stable
financing for basic research, more concern for advancing
knowledge for its own sake. We mean cooperation with

other communities of scholars and creative thinkers, as in the International Geophysical Year, in order that our pursuit of truth may be an adventure we share with all mankind. And we mean that the pursuit of truth in itself is the highest activity of man.

Here, then, in all its ramifications of expense, of standards, content and opportunity is a top priority for a great new America and a national purpose few would dispute.

I would include not far below a reconsideration of our urban life. We are adding a city the size of Philadelphia to our population every year. From every large urban center the suburbs spread out and out, without shape or grace or any centered form of civic life. Many are so built that they are the slums of tomorrow. Meanwhile, town centers decay, racial divisions destroy harmony, commuters jam the city approaches, and a strange, half-life of divided families and Sunday fathers is growing up. If we accept both the fact of our rapid growth in population and the fact that most people will live in cities, we can begin a serious attack upon our congested, ugly, inconvenient metropolitan sprawls—creating the preconditions of a good urban life that could become a new model for an urbanizing world. In this vital field of future living the Russian contribution is meager, but we will find, as at Brasilia, that others are plunging forward ahead of us.

Restoration of compassion is a clumsy way to describe another great embracing national purpose. In the past, evils and miseries have been the driving force of majority discontent. But now for the first time in history, the engine of social progress has run out of the fuel of discontent. We have therefore to mobilize our imagination, our personal sense of indignity and outrage, if we are to act on the conviction that gross poverty, curable illness, racial indignity, mental disease, and suffering in old age are a disgrace amidst the surrounding luxuries, privileges and indulgence of such a wealthy society as ours.

And here our top priorities must reach beyond our shores. For it is not chiefly in America or in the fortunate North Atlantic basin that the world's miseries are to be found. On the contrary, we confidently predict to ourselves a doubling and tripling of our high living standards. But in Asia, Africa and Latin America live scores of millions who, on present forecasts, can equally confidently expect to fare steadily worse. This disparity in living standards between the rich and the poor is as great a threat to peace as the arms race, and narrowing the gap as imperative as arms control.

The purpose of our aid programs should therefore be designed not primarily to counter Communism—though it will do this too—but to create conditions of self-respect and self-sustaining growth in economies still behind the threshold of modernization. The needs are so staggering that to achieve this national purpose will demand not only the greatest intelligence, perseverance and financial enterprise, private and public, but also a much broader cooperation and joint effort with other advanced nations than in the past. But if we accept this as fundamental American foreign policy, not on a year to year basis but for the next critical generation, we shall develop the perspective and staying power to reach real solutions, not doles, handouts, bad debts—and dislike.

And in doing so, we shall do more than set the processes of modernization in healthy motion. I believe that this is the chief way to us to extend our vision of "a more perfect union" to all mankind. It is a commonplace that in a world made one by science and the atom, the old national boundaries are dissolving, the old landmarks vanishing. We can't have privacy and the hydrogen bomb too. A workable human society has to be fashioned and we must start where we can—by setting up the institutions of a common economic life, by employing our wealth and wisdom to spark the growth of production in poorer lands, by working together with like-minded powers to establish the permanent patterns of a workable world economy. In this way we can hope to establish one of the two main preconditions of peaceful human society—economic solidarity and mutual help.

The other precondition of peace—and this, of all priorities is our highest—is our unwavering search for peace under law which, in our present context, means controlled and supervised disarmament. Only a disarmed world offers us security worth the name any longer.

I do not believe, even now, that the world accepts the idea that genuine disarmament is America's primary, public purpose. We talk of peace and our devotion to it. But there is far more hard, unremitting effort in the task than speeches or protestations or journeys—however distant. What seems to be lacking is sincere and sustained dedication to this goal and unwearying pursuit by our highest officers, military and civilian, in season and out. As it is now no major conference occurs without preliminary rumors of American indecision and even suggestions that our leaders are "dragging their feet." I would wish instead to see created an international atmosphere in which such forays as Mr. Khrushchev's speech on total disarmament at the United Nations would fall like a

lead balloon from the certain knowledge all round the
world that this and nothing less had been for years the
public policy of the United States.

*   *   *

I believe that the American people are prepared to face
the cost, the rigors, the efforts and the challenge which are
involved in recovering the public image of a great America.
The cost in physical terms—in hard work, in discipline, in
more taxes if need be—is hard to estimate precisely. Any
arms control would release resources. Our growing national product will certainly provide wider margins out
of which vital public expenditure could be met. But if the
cost is higher than our present level of public spending,
I frankly believe that education and health for our children, dignity and beauty in our civic lives, and security
and well-being in the world at large, are more important
than the "things" which might otherwise have priority.

But still more important is America's need to face
squarely the *facts* about its situation. If freedom is really
the organizing principle of our society, then we cannot
forget that it is not illusion, propaganda and sedatives, but
truth, and truth alone, that makes us free. Under the
influence of the politics of sedation and the techniques of
salesmanship I believe that in recent years self-deceit has
slackened our grip on reality. We have tended to shirk the
difficult truth and accept the easy half-truth. Perhaps it is
always that way; as the old humorist Josh Billings used to
say: "As scarce as truth is, the supply is always greater than
the demand."

But we know from our own lives that reality entails
hard choices and disappointments: that it measures real

achievement not in terms of luck but in terms of difficulties overcome. I don't believe our national life can follow any other pattern.

No preordained destiny decrees that America shall have all the breaks and soft options. Neither greatness nor even freedom lies that way. So we must surely return to the reality principle, to the bracing, invigorating, upland climate of truth itself. I think we are ready now to move forward into the rigors and glories of the new decade with open eyes, eager step and firm purposes worthy of our great past.

III

"We Have Purpose . . . We All Know It"

Archibald MacLeish

THAT SOMETHING HAS GONE WRONG IN AMERICA MOST OF US know. We are richer than any nation before us. We have more Things in our garages and kitchens and cellars than Louis Quatorze had in the whole of Versailles. We have come nearer to the suppression of grinding poverty than even the 19th Century Utopians thought seriously possible. We have wiped out many of the pests and scourges which afflicted humanity. We have lengthened men's lives and protected their infancy. We have advanced science to the edges of the inexplicable and hoisted our technology to the sun itself.

We are in a state of growth and flux and change in which cities flow out into countryside and countryside moves into cities and new industries are born and old industries vanish and the customs of generations alter and fathers speak different languages from their sons. In brief, we are prosperous, lively, successful, inventive, diligent—but, nevertheless and notwithstanding, something is wrong and we know it.

The trouble seems to be that we don't feel right with ourselves or with the country. It isn't only the Russians. We have outgrown the adolescent time when everything that was wrong with America was the fault of the Russians and all we needed to do to be saved was to close the State Department and keep the Communists out of motion pictures. It isn't just the Russians now: it's ourselves. It's the way we feel about ourselves as Americans. We feel that we've lost our way in the woods, that we don't know where we are going—if anywhere.

I agree—but I still feel that the diagnosis is curious, for the fact is, of course, that we *have* a national purpose—the most precisely articulated national purpose in recorded history—and that we all know it. It is the purpose put into words by the most lucid mind of that most lucid century, the 18th, and adopted on the Fourth of July in 1776 as a declaration of the existence and national intent of a new nation.

Not only is it a famous statement of purpose: it is also an admirable statement of purpose. Prior to July 4, 1776, the national purpose of nations had been to dominate: to dominate at least their neighbors and rivals and, wherever possible, to dominate the world. The American national purpose was the opposite: to liberate from domination; to set men free.

All men, to Thomas Jefferson, were created equal. *All*

men were endowed by their Creator with certain inalienable rights. Among these rights were life, liberty and the pursuit of happiness. It was the existence of these rights which justified American independence from King George and justified also the revolution which would have to be fought for that independence. It was the existence of these rights which would provide a foundation for the government to be established when independence was secure.

We not only *have* a national purpose: we have a national purpose of such aspiration, such potentiality, such power of hope that we refer to it—or used to—as the American Dream. We were dedicated from our beginnings to the proposition that we existed not merely to exist but to be free, and the dedication was real in spite of the fact that it took us three generations and a bloody war to practice our preachment within our own frontiers. It was real in spite of the fact that its practice is still a delusion in numerous pockets of hypocrisy across the nation.

To be free is not, perhaps, a political program in the modern sense, but from the point of view of a new nation it may be something better. The weakness of political programs—Five Year Plans and the like—is that they can be achieved. But human freedom can never be achieved because human freedom is a continuously evolving condition. It is infinite in its possibilities—as infinite as the human soul which it enfranchises. The nation which seeks it and persists in its search will move through history as a ship moves on a compass course toward a constantly opening horizon.

And America did move steadily on before it lost headway in the generation in which we live. The extraordinary feel of liveness which the Americans communicated, whether agreeably or not, to their early European visitors came from that sense of national expectation. We were never a very philosophical people politically after Jefferson and his contemporaries left us. We were practical men who took instruction from the things we saw and heard and did. But the purpose defined in our Declaration was a reality to us notwithstanding. It gave us *aim* as the continent gave us *scope,* and the old American character with its almost anarchic passion for idiosyncrasy and difference was the child of both. Those Missouri militiamen Parkman describes in *The Oregon Trail* slogging their way West to the war with Mexico, each in his own rig and each in his own way, could have constituted an army nowhere else. When, at Sacramento, a drunken officer commanded his company to halt and a private yelled "Charge!" the company charged, knocking five times their number of Mexicans out of prepared entrenchments. The anarchy didn't matter because they were all headed in the same direction and the name of that direction was West—or freedom. They had a future in common and they had a purpose in common and the purpose was the enfranchisement of men—of all men—to think for themselves, speak for themselves, govern themselves, pursue happiness for themselves and so become themselves.

Why then do we need to rediscover what our national purpose is? Because the words of the Declaration in its superb housing in the National Archives have become archival words, words out of history? Because the Bill of Rights of the American Constitution belongs, like the Magna Carta, in an airtight case? No one who reads the newspapers could think so. There has never been a time when courts and Congress devoted more of their attention

to the constitutional guarantees of individual freedom
than they do today, and as for the Declaration of Independence, its language is more alive in the middle of the
20th Century than it was in the middle of the 19th or even
when it was written. It is not Communism, however Communism may attempt to exploit them, which has begotten
the new nations of Asia and Africa or the new nationalistic
stirrings in South America and the Caribbean and even in
Europe. The Marxist dream is a dream of economic machinery, not of living men: of a universal order and system,
not a proliferation of nationalities. No, the dream which
has set the jungle and the cane on fire is different and
older. It is Thomas Jefferson's dream—the dream which
he and his contemporaries believed would change the
world. It *is* changing the world—and not later than one
might expect. Two hundred years is a short time in the
history of institutions.

If the American Dream is out of date today it is out of
date only in America—only in America and in the Communist countries in which the political police have extin-
guished it. But is it really out of date in America? Is its
power to direct and draw us really so faint that we are lost
in the blaze of our own prosperity and must enlist the aid
of learned men to tell us where the future lies? That, I
think, is a question for debate in these discussions.

Have we lost our sense of purpose or have we merely
lost touch with it? Have we rejected the arduous labor to
which our beginnings committed us? Or are we merely
confused and bewildered by the volcanic upheavals which
have changed the landscapes of our lives? Or is it neither
rejection nor confusion? Is it nothing more than the
flatulence and fat of an overfed people whose children pre-

pare at the milk-shake counter for coronary occlusions in middle age? Are we simply too thick through the middle to dream?

I doubt for myself that we have rejected the American Dream or have even thought of rejecting it. There are minorities, of course, who have little enthusiasm for the actualities of the American commitment to freedom, but this is largely because they do not understand what the struggle it culminated was all about. Certain areas on the fringes of Europe were preserved by their geographical location from the necessity of living through the crisis of the Western mind which we call the Reformation, and American stock from these areas tends to find the master-mistress idea of the American Revolution—the idea which raised it from a minor war for independence to a world event—incomprehensible if not actually misguided. It is not a question of religion. Catholics from the heart of the European continent understand Jefferson as well as any Protestant. It is a question of geography. Men and women whose ancestors were not obliged to fight the battle for or against freedom of conscience cannot for the life of them understand why censorship should be considered evil or why authority is not preferable to freedom.

But all this does not add up to a rejection of the American dedication to liberty—the American dedication to the enfranchisement of the human spirit. The Irish Catholics, who are among the most persistent and politically powerful advocates of increasing censorship in the U.S., and who are brought up to submit to clerical authority in matters which the American tradition reserves to the individual conscience, are nevertheless among the most fervent of American patriots. And if their enthusiasm for freedom of the mind is restrained, their passion for freedom of the man is glorious. Only if a separate system of education should be used to perpetuate the historical ignorance and moral obtuseness on which fear of freedom of the mind is based would the danger of the rejection of the American Dream from this quarter become serious. As for the rest, the only wholehearted rejection comes from the Marxists with their curiously childish notion that it is more realistic and more intelligent to talk about economic machinery than about men. But the Marxists, both Mr. Hoovers to the contrary notwithstanding, have no perceptible influence on American opinion.

I cannot believe that we have *rejected* the purpose on which our Republic was founded. Neither can I believe that our present purposelessness results from our economic fat and our spiritual indolence. It is not because we are too comfortable that the dream has left us. It is true, I suppose, that we eat better—at least more—than any nation ever has. It is true too that there are streaks of American fat, some of it very ugly fat, and that it shows most unbecomingly at certain points in New York and Miami and along the California coast. But the whole country is not lost in a sluggish, sun-oiled sleep beneath a beach umbrella, dreaming of More and More. We have our share, and more than our share, of mink coats and prestige cars and expense account restaurants and oil millionaires, but America is not made of such things as these. We are an affluent society but we are not affluent to the point of spiritual sloth.

Most American young women, almost regardless of income, work harder in their homes and with their children than their mothers or their grandmothers had to. For one thing, domestic servants have all but disappeared and no machine can cook a meal or mind a baby. For another, there are more babies than there have been for generations. For still another, the rising generation is better educated than its parents were and more concerned with the serious business of life—the life of the mind. To watch your daughter-in-law taking care of her own house, bringing up four children, running the Parent-Teacher Association, singing in the church choir and finding time nevertheless to read the books she wants to read and hear the music she wants to hear and see the plays she can afford to, is a salutory thing. She may think more about machines and gadgets than you ever did but that is largely because there are more machines and gadgets to think about. No one who has taught, as I have been doing for the past 10 years, can very seriously doubt that the generation on the way up is more intelligent than the generation now falling back. And as for the materialism about which we talk so much, it is worth remembering that the popular whipping boy of the moment among the intelligent young is precisely "Madison Avenue," that the mythical advertising copy writer who is supposed to persuade us to wallow in cosmetics and tail-fin cars. We may be drowning in Things, but the best of our sons and daughters like it even less than we do.

What then has gone wrong? The answer, I submit, is fairly obvious and will be found where one would expect to find it: in the two great wars which have changed so much beside. The first world war altered not only our position in the world but our attitude toward ourselves and toward our business as a people. Having won a war to "make the world safe for democracy," we began to act as though democracy itself had been won—as though there was nothing left for us to do but enjoy ourselves: make money in the stock market, gin in the bathtub and whoopee in the streets. The American journey had been completed. The American goal was reached. We had emerged from the long trek westward to find ourselves on the Plateau of Permanent Prosperity. We were *there!* It took the disaster of 1929 and the long depression which followed to knock the fantasy out of our heads but the damage had been done. We had lost touch with the driving force of our own history.

The effect of the second war was different—and the same. The second war estranged us from our genius as a people. We fought it because we realized that our dream of human liberty could not survive in the slave state Hitler was imposing on the world. We won it with no such illusions as had plagued us 25 years before: there was another more voracious slave state behind Hitler's. But though we did not repeat the folly of the '20s we repeated the delusion of the '20s. We acted again as though freedom were an accomplished fact. We no longer thought of it as safe but we made a comparable mistake: we thought of it as something which could be protected by building walls around it, by "containing" its enemy.

But the truth is, of course, that freedom is never an accomplished fact. It is always a process. Which is why the drafters of the Declaration spoke of the *pursuit* of happiness: they knew their Thucydides and therefore knew that "the secret of happiness is freedom and the secret of freedom, courage." The only way freedom can be defended is not by fencing it in but by enlarging it, exercising it. Though we did defend freedom by exercising it through the Marshall Plan in Europe, we did not, for understand-able reasons involving the colonial holdings of our allies, defend freedom by exercising it in Asia and Africa where the future is about to be decided.

The results have been hurtful to the world and to our-selves. How hurtful they have been to the world we can see in Cuba where a needed and necessary and hopeful revolution against an insufferable dictatorship appears to have chosen the Russian solution of its economic difficulties rather than ours. We have tried to explain that ominous fact to ourselves in the schoolgirl vocabulary of the McCarthy years, saying that Castro and his friends are Communists. But whether they are or not—and the charge is at least unproved—there is no question whatever of the enormous popular support for their regime and for as much of their program as is now known. Not even those who see Communist conspiracies underneath everyone else's bed have contended that the Cuban people were tricked or policed into their enthusiasm for their revolu-tion. On the contrary the people appear to outrun the government in their eagerness for the new order. What this means is obvious. What this means is that the wave of the future, to the great majority of Cubans, is the Russian wave, not the American. That fact, and its implications for the rest of Latin America, to say nothing of Africa and Asia, is the fact we should be looking at, hard and long. If the Russian purpose seems more vigorous and more promising to the newly liberated peoples of the world than the American purpose, then we have indeed lost the "battle for men's minds" of which we talk so much.

As for ourselves, the hurt has been precisely the loss of a sense of national purpose. To engage, as we have over the past 15 years, in programs having as their end and aim not action to further a purpose of our own but *counter*action to frustrate a purpose of the Russians is to invite just such a state of mind. A nation cannot be sure even of its own identity when it finds itself associated in country after country—as we have most recently in South Korea and Turkey—with regimes whose political practices are inimical to its own.

What, then, is the issue in this debate? What is the problem? Not to *discover* our national purpose but to *exercise* it. Which means, ultimately, to exercise it for its own sake, not for the defeat of those who have a different purpose. There is all the difference in the world between strengthening the enemies of our enemies because they are against what we are against, and supporting the hopes of mankind because we too believe in them, because they are our hopes also. The fields of action in the two cases may be the same: Africa and Asia and Latin America. The tools of action—military assistance and above all economic and industrial and scientific aid—may look alike. But the actions will be wholly different. The first course of action surrenders initiative to the Russians and accepts the Russian hypothesis that Communism is the new force moving in the world. The second asserts what is palpably true, that the new force moving in the world is the force we set in motion, the force which gave us, almost two centuries ago, our liberating mission. The first is costly, as we know. The second will be more costly still. But the second, because it recaptures for the cause of freedom the initiative which belongs to it and restores to the country the confidence it has lost, is capable of succeeding. The first, because it can never be anything but a policy of resistance, can only continue to resist and to accomplish nothing more.

There are those, I know, who will reply that the liberation of humanity, the freedom of man and mind, is nothing but a dream. They are right. It is. It is the American dream.

IV

"Turn the Cold War Tide in America's Favor"

DAVID SARNOFF

THE UNFOLDING AMERICAN DEBATE ON NATIONAL PURPOSE carries the disquieting implication that our traditional purposes, though they served the nation well in the past, have somehow been outmoded if not wholly invalidated. This I do not believe to be true. I am convinced, on the contrary, that these time-tested purposes, rooted in the nation's whole history, are more compelling than ever before. More, they are indispensable in enabling the U.S. to meet the paramount challenge of this epoch: the struggle between Communism and freedom. If revitalized, redefined for our times and translated into great decisions, they could turn the tide of conflict in our favor.

The need now, as I see it, is not for tailor-made new

purposes but for a renewed understanding and dedication to old purposes—raised to a dimension adequate for this fateful period. The need is for firm and inspiring positions commensurate with the immense perils facing our country and the human race.

The Communists, whatever their tactics in a given period, have never deviated from *their* purpose. It has been openly proclaimed from Lenin's day down to Khrushchev's and Mao Tse-tung's. It is, in the words of the official Moscow magazine *Kommunist,* "implacable struggle" looking to "the inevitable end of capitalism and the total triumph of Communism." Such a challenge can be met and frustrated only with a purpose of equal scope.

Five years ago I submitted a memorandum to the White House sketching a Program for a Political Offensive against World Communism. "For Moscow," it said, "the real alternative to a nuclear showdown is not 'peace' but political-psychological warfare of a magnitude to weaken, demoralize, chip away and ultimately take over what remains of the free world." The memorandum therefore urged that we renounce all delusions of easy solutions and compromises; that instead we mount a *political counter-strategy* as massive, as intensive and as clear about its ultimate goals as the strategy of the enemy himself.

Events in the intervening years and intensified Communist pressures today have, if anything, fortified this point of view. The essence of my proposed program, for which I claim no originality, was—and still is—an unequivocal decision to fight the so-called cold war with a will and on a scale for complete victory.

The decision would have to be communicated to the entire world as boldly and energetically as the Communists communicate their intentions. Our message to humankind must be that America has decided, irrevocably, to win the cold war and thereby to cancel out the destructive power of Soviet-based Communism. A national commitment of this scope, I submit, would be consistent with American instincts and experience, a restatement of historic purposes in contemporary terms.

The nature of those purposes has been sufficiently defined by the editors in the introductory article to this series. It is explicit in basic American documents, beginning with the Declaration of Independence of which Thomas Jefferson could say, "We are acting for all mankind."

It is implicit in the widespread assertion—presented by some as an accusation—that our foreign policies have been "idealistic." Through the generations Americans have always thought of themselves as being in the vanguard of freedom. They cherished the image of their country as the citadel of democracy and morality and a living defiance to despotism anywhere.

The Rockefeller Brothers Fund Report on U.S. Foreign Policy—prepared by a panel of which I was a member and published last year—put it this way: "The United States at its best has always seen its national life as an experiment in liberty . . . [Americans] have known that the hopes of the world were, in some measure, bound up with their success. . . . Whenever [the United States] has wielded effective power in the world, its ideals and its moral convictions have played a vital part in its decisions. Whenever, on the contrary, the United States has tried to act without moral conviction, or in ways that went counter to its basic beliefs, it has found itself inhibited and has ultimately had to rechart its course. . . . Ideas and ideals are thus to the United States an essential element of reality."

This is why expediency and appeasement, solutions that condemn other peoples to enslavement, failure to react to international crimes violate the deepest instincts of the American people. Why is there such a pervasive skepticism about our historic purposes and such a widespread search for substitutes? Why the shrinking from lofty goals for all mankind in favor of the safe, the compromising, or mere survival?

The easy answer—that it is all due to the advent of terrible new weapons—will hardly do. The calendar refutes it: the retreat began before those weapons were forged and grew more panicky during the time when America had a monopoly on the atom bomb. It was precisely in the years before Soviet Russia produced the bomb that Communism scored its greatest gains, and it did so almost always by the default of the free world. The Soviet advantages were not military and technological but political and psychological.

The true answer, as I see it, is related to the ever-rising costs of idealism in terms of the sacrifices and the hazards involved. The trouble is not that the older purposes have become irrelevant but that they have become too relevant. I mean that the time when America could serve passively as an example or inspiration to other nations has run out. Today, professions of principle have serious consequences: they must be implemented in policy and action. To say it in slang, the time has come to put up or shut up.

As far as the contest with Communism is concerned we had "shut up," quite literally. We had curbed our tongues for fear of offending the delicate sensibilities of those who daily offend *us*. Few democratic leaders dare to speak as uninhibitedly about the coming doom of the Communist empire as Khrushchev and Mao Tse-tung regularly speak about our impending doom. Our opponents defy, denounce and challenge, while we plead and propitiate. We have left the vocabulary of confidence and victory to the other side, contenting ourselves with such solacing and temporizing words as accommodation, *modus vivendi,* relaxed tensions and coexistence.

This semantic timidity, of course, is merely a symptom and a minor one. The all-encompassing malady is a loss of nerve, marked by depleted self-esteem and purpose. It has impelled us, whenever we have been faced with a choice of interpretations on some aspect of the Communist affliction, to choose the more agreeable one, the one more conducive to complacency and less likely to tax our courage. With rare exceptions the choice has turned out to be the wrong and often the disastrous one, regardless of the political parties in power in this country and in the free world.

Thus in the 1930s we eagerly found assurance in Stalin's talk about "socialism in one country." Later we relaxed in the cozy conviction that the Chinese Communists were simply "agrarian reformers." We prefer to believe in the "evolution" of Communism, though there has not been the slightest revision of ultimate Communist goals. We seek a comforting answer to our prayers in tensions between Moscow and Peking, though these are strictly within the framework of their unshakable alliance against the West, no more significant than Anglo-American tension within our alliance.

A familiar gambit is to list Communism as just one item in a long inventory of problems. But if the Sino-Soviet bloc wins world dominion, the other problems will cease to matter: they will have been solved for the free world in about the way that death solves all bodily ills.

In the debate on National Purpose we find at least one area of virtually unanimous agreement. It is that sheer survival, in the elementary physical sense, is not enough. A nation that thinks and acts exclusively for self-preservation cannot, in the present-day world, preserve itself. The posture, even if it were desired or desirable, has been turned into an anachronism by the surge of science and technology. The world has become too small for physical, economic or political isolationism. The polarization of forces dueling for supremacy has gone too far to permit the survival of an island of humanism in a sea of dehumanized totalitarianism. No single nation can survive unless the civilization of which it is part survives.

Our civilization, too, cannot remain isolated, confined to a delimited segment of the earth and indifferent to the humanity beyond those limits. The world cannot be frozen in its present patterns. In this period of great flux and of intermeshed revolutions, static and passive arrangements are doomed to disruption. If the area of freedom is not expanded, then assuredly it will continue to contract.

Despite this, "survival of the free world"—side by side with an unfree world—has been and remains the maximum goal of Western diplomacy. Not the weakening and eventual defeat of Communism but a lasting accommodation seems to mark the farthest reach of hope. It is scarcely a vision to inspire confidence or zeal, and in any case it is utterly utopian, because two parties are needed to make an accommodation.

The best analysis of Communist strategy that I know is

in a recent book called *Protracted Conflict* by Dr. Robert Strausz-Hupé of the University of Pennsylvania and three associates. The book's title is a phrase used by Mao Tse-tung. The Communist plan, say the authors, is protracted in time and space and in the limitless variety of its techniques and weapons, and the weapons can even include "the final and total knockout punch." Short of surrender, the authors see for our world no alternative but a many-sided, continuous, long-range counteroffensive.

Such a policy would reject all illusions of an enduring truce, let alone a negotiated division of the globe. The historic contest will be with us for a long, long time. We may delay, maneuver, bargain and compromise, but it will be so much flailing of water unless all such moves become for us—as they have always been for the enemy—calculated holding actions geared to long-range objectives, means not ends, tactics not strategy.

Whatever we do or fail to do in the years and decades ahead, we shall be forced to take great risks and make great sacrifices. These cannot be evaded even by piecemeal surrenders. In fact, if Americans and other free peoples are to understand and accept these costs and exertions, there must be some rational relation between the magnitude of the goal and the magnitude of the burdens it imposes.

This means that in the conflict with Communism we must become the dynamic challenger rather than remain the inert target of challenge. Only then can freedom regain the initiative. Only then will we have a global goal to match that of Communism, and the incentive to apply the full weight of our brains, energies and resources to its achievement. The great decision, once made and communicated to all concerned, will dictate its appropriate program of policy and action. The strategy will shape the necessary tactics.

Even the things we are now doing and must continue to do will become more relevant and more effective when geared to a conscious ultimate goal. Military and economic aid to our allies, to underdeveloped areas and to neutral nations will cease to be hit-or-miss improvisations. They will be integral elements of an affirmative program. Propaganda, cultural exchanges, diplomatic moves, summit meetings will all acquire for us—as they always have for the Communists—dimensions of purpose beyond their limited immediate effects.

Before the Soviet Union attained its present technological stature, America's paramount problem appeared to be the struggle for men's minds. Today it is dangerous to concentrate on any one facet of the conflict. I think of the image in terms of a table with four legs, military, political, economic and psychological. The significance of the last three is self-evident, since they relate to activities short of all-out war. But the "military leg" must not be underrated.

The present approximate balance of terror presents a false appearance of stability. But it may be upset. And if we relax in this area it will be upset. The enemy is constantly probing our vitality and resolution. Any one of these probes may lead to the brink of war and possibly to war itself. No matter how often we repeat that war is "unthinkable" it remains possible. War may be touched off by accident, or it may come because the Communist high command considers itself ready to deliver the "final and total knockout punch." The maintenance of adequate military power, both offensive and defensive, is therefore of paramount importance. Whether it is ever used or not, moreover, it is the indispensable shield for all other types of action in the protracted conflict.

A strategy for victory in the cold war would, however, begin with a complete reappraisal of present efforts. It would aim to seize the initiative in every possible arena of competition. Not merely the expansion of present projects and the addition of new ones would be considered but how to give each of them a clear role within the framework of the over-all objective.

It would not reject courses of action simply because they are unconventional. We would no longer disdain to use against the enemy some of the weapons used against us. Having finally acknowledged that the struggle is decisive and therefore as real as a "real" war, we would not hesitate to fight fire with fire.

American ingenuity would be called upon to evolve devices and techniques to exploit weaknesses and vulnerabilities in the Communist world, to keep the enemy constantly off balance, to impose upon him problems and crises instead of always waiting to counteract crises of his making. By all the instruments of communication and through the loudspeakers of events, we would aim to saturate the Communist world with reminders that we intend to keep alive the memory of human dignity, the hatred of injustice, the hope of liberation and the courage needed for resistance.

Debates in the United Nations and at diplomatic conferences would be made sounding boards for our views as well as for theirs. No allusion to "colonialism" would be permitted to pass without our throwing the limelight

on Red imperialism and on the principles of self-deter-
mination.

Thus the Communist world, rather than ours, would
tend increasingly to become the principal battlefield of
ideological and political conflict. The immunity their
world has so long enjoyed would be shattered.

A bill to establish a Freedom Academy for training cold
war specialists—what a LIFE editorial called a Political
West Point—is before Congress. Whatever the merits or
demerits of this particular bill, it is in line with a commitment to victory. Various proposals have been made for
setting up a Liberation Force, a volunteer formation drawn
largely from among refugees from captive nations and
ready to serve in emergencies. That, too, is in line with a
strategy for victory. Official and private agencies of other
kinds would be generated by focused strategic thinking in
offensive rather than defensive terms. And a new department of Cabinet rank could and should be established to
plan and coordinate all cold war activities.

Certainly this new approach would call for substantial
sacrifices in material terms. But the notion that it would
require a deep cut in American living standards under-
estimates the wealth and productive genius of our country.
The more demanding sacrifices, indeed, would be in the
psychological and moral domains. Our people, in short,
would have to renounce complacency, euphoria and illusion; they would have to embrace the grim but inspiring
realities of our epoch.

The ultimate rise of a world order under law is dictated
by the logic of devastating weaponry, the conquest of space,
and modern communications. What remains to be settled

is whether it will be an order rooted in freedom or in universal tyranny.

I do not doubt that we have what it takes to assure that it will be an order that we may cherish. The Western concepts of open societies, of liberty under law, of government by the consent of the governed, of the supremacy of the individual rather than the state—these are far closer to the natural aspirations of man than the anthill concepts of Communism. In any equal propaganda contest, what these Western concepts have brought in human well-being will become obvious and irresistible to the majority of mankind.

In my 1955 Memorandum to the White House I wrote: "Once that decision is made, some of the means for implementing it will become self-evident; others will be explored and developed under the impetus of a clear-cut goal. Agreement on the problem must come before agreement on the solution." But Abraham Lincoln said it better a century ago: "Determine that the thing can and shall be done, and then we shall find the way."

V

"Men Must Be Changed Before a Nation Can"

Billy Graham

A FEW MONTHS AGO I PLAYED GOLF WITH A MAN WHO looked and acted as though he enjoyed perfect health. Today he is dead. In spite of outward appearance he had a virulent form of cancer which within a short time took his life.

I am convinced that regardless of the outward appearance of prosperity within the corporate life of America today there is present a form of moral and spiritual cancer which could ultimately lead to the country's destruction unless the disease is treated promptly and the trend reversed.

Many thoughtful Americans are disturbed because as a nation we seem bereft of a sense of purpose. We have the mood and stance of a people who have "arrived" and have nowhere else to go.

We have achieved an affluence unprecedented in our history.

Some of our most outstanding citizens are warning us with statements that are reminiscent of the flaming prophets of old who prophesied the doom of nations that refused to change their moral course. George F. Kennan, the historian and former American ambassador to Russia, recently said, "If you ask me whether a country—with no highly developed sense of national purpose, with the overwhelming accent of life on personal comfort, with a dearth of public services and a surfeit of privately sold gadgetry, with insufficient social discipline even to keep its major industries functioning without grievous interruption—if you ask me whether such a country has, over the long run, good chances of competing with a purposeful, serious and disciplined society such as that of the Soviet Union, I must say that the answer is No."

Many American leaders have serious doubts concerning the nation's moral and spiritual capability to match the challenge of a dedicated, disciplined Communism. I am convinced that unless we heed the warning, unless we bring Americans back to an awareness of God's moral laws, unless a moral fiber is put back into the structure of our nation, we are headed for national disaster.

No patient is willing to take the doctor's medicine until he has heard the diagnosis, and no one should try to prescribe a national purpose for America until he has listened to her heart. It has been my privilege to travel and preach in nearly all the states of the country for 10 years. I have talked personally with thousands of Americans from every walk of life. My own feeling is that the heart of America is still basically sound but that the blood stream is being poisoned with the toxins of modern life.

History has many examples of nations that "arrived" and then fell due to overconfidence, internal decay or neglect of the ideals and philosophies that had made them great. America is in desperate need of a moral and spiritual transfusion that will cause her to recapture some of the strength and idealism that made us the greatest nation in the world.

First, we need to recapture the strength of individualism. Mass-produced machinery has given rise to the mass-produced man. We are inclined to think like the Joneses, dress like the Joneses, build houses like the Joneses and talk like the Joneses. We have become status conscious and have built for ourselves sets of status symbols.

A few weeks ago, in a visit to the Holy Land, I followed in the steps of some of the great nonconformists of the Bible, men such as Elijah, Amos, Micah. I stood on top of Mount Carmel, overlooking the beautiful Israeli city of Haifa, and prayed, "Lord, help me not to be a conformist." Psychologists tell us that we are shaped by heredity and by environment. The prophets of Israel were a part of their environment, yet they were not shaped by it. They reacted *against* it. They had the courage to stand for moral right—alone if necessary. We need men who will live up to their idealism and who refuse to be moral copycats.

Second, we need to recapture the spirit of '76. While we encourage nationalism for ambitious smaller nations abroad, we discourage it at home. Patriotism in America seems to be "old hat." If a man gets out and waves the American flag, he is now "suspect" or called a "reactionary." We applaud the nationalistic demonstrations in other countries. Perhaps we need a few demonstrations for America. The Soviet Communist party recently published 97 slogans for May Day with the accent on complete liquidation of colonialism and a production drive to overtake the United States. Where are the American slogans? Commander Vincent J. Lonergan, a Roman Catholic chaplain, warned participants at the White House Conference on Children and Youth recently that "far too many of [our youth] have been led to believe that patriotism is a phony virtue, that military service is an intolerable burden to be avoided as a plague; or if imposed upon them, to be carried out grudgingly, without pride, without honor. It is extremely important that we imbue our young people with the spirit of intelligent sacrifice that is our heritage as Americans." What a heartening thing it would be to see the people of America making the spirit of '76 the spirit of 1960.

Third, we need to recapture hardness and discipline in our national life. Our excessive allotment of leisure in an affluent society is making dullards out of us. Thousands of our young men are not even able to pass the army physical exam. We play too much and work too little. We overeat, overdrink, oversex and overplay, but few of us are ever overexercised. We have become surfeited in this land of plenty. Our sedentary way of life has brought an alarming rash of coronaries and related illnesses. We may be the richest people in the world, but we are far from being the sturdiest.

The Bible warns, "Woe to them that are at ease in Zion." We need to recapture the love and dedication of hard work.

Fourth, we must recapture the courage of our fathers. The chairman of the history department of one of our great universities recently confided in me, "We have become a nation of cowards." I challenged him on this statement, but his arguments were convincing. The great courage that once was so characteristic of America and Americans seems to be going. Many of our military leaders are deeply concerned about the disappearance of the will to fight for what we believe. We seem to be content to sit within the security of our homes and watch the brave Western heroes on television doing the things that inwardly we wish we had the courage to do. What boldness we may have is vicarious and reflected in the fictional acts on the screen. We are content to live in a world of fantasy and cringe at the thought of becoming personally involved with life. We are so intent on saving our own skins that we are in danger of losing our souls.

We have become reluctant to follow a course that isn't popular, even if deep inside we know it is right. If the odds are ten to one in our favor we will take a stand, but if there is any appreciable risk involved in standing up for what we know to be right, we'll play it safe. Woodrow Wilson said, "I would a great deal rather lose in a cause that I know someday will triumph than triumph in a cause that I know someday will lose." We have played the flip side of that record and said, "I won't buck the tide of popular opinion, for I would rather be liked than to be right." This is the sort of devastating fear that eats at the heart of a people and robs them of a sense of individual and national purpose.

Fifth, we must recapture the American challenge. William James 50 years ago observed that America needs "a moral equivalent of war" to challenge it. The rise of the Beatniks is at least partially a pitiful attempt to find a challenge. Robert Lindner, the late Baltimore psycho-analyst, wrote the book *Rebel without a Cause*. Lindner found that American youth feel that they are so surrounded by conformity that they rebel for the sake of rebelling. This is the psychological basis of much of our teen-age delinquency. We need a challenge such as our forefathers had when they transformed this wilderness into a civilized nation. While the challenge of the present hour may take different forms, I believe it is even greater than what the early Americans faced.

What is the American challenge? What is our reason for existence? There are a thousand challenges that should stir our emotions and demand the dedication of every fiber of our being. Some of them may be:

► The challenge to be on the side of the little people of the world, the hungry, the homeless, the friendless, the oppressed, the discriminated against, the captives and those who live in countries where there is no freedom.

► The challenge to throw political expediency to the wind if necessary and do what we know is morally right because it is right.

► The challenge of sharing our immense wealth with others.

► The challenge of electing men with moral courage to high office who will be ruthless with the gangsters that operate on such a wide scale throughout the nation.

► The challenge of selling the American dream and ideals to the world.

► The challenge of humility to admit our failures, to repent of our sins and to unashamedly serve God.

► The challenge of solving the worldwide problems of ignorance, disease and poverty.

► The challenge of finding the individual peace and joy that is so lacking in the "good life" of modern America.

► The challenge of contentment with what we have, remembering the words of the Apostle Paul, "I have learned that in whatsoever state I find myself therewith to be content."

America still has a glorious future if we rise to the challenges, opportunities and responsibilities of the hour. If we fail, may God help us!

Sixth, we must recapture our moral strength and our faith in God. Some recent surveys of American life have been alarming and discouraging. We now know that cheating is accepted practice in our society. Morals have become irrelevant or relative—no longer are there moral absolutes. Success at any price is our maxim. We excuse our immorality by saying, "Everybody is doing it." Many of our modern educators have decreed that we are what we are because of external pressures and that each of us is a victim of environment or inherent tendencies and that we cannot help what we are. This is totally contrary to the teachings of Holy Scripture. The Bible teaches that we are responsible for our moral choices.

We cannot possibly exist if we reject the time-honored moral absolutes of the Ten Commandments and the Sermon on the Mount. The Scripture says, "Righteousness exalteth a nation, but sin is a reproach to any people."

The nation is no longer shocked at exposés. Our conscience is being hardened and the Scriptures warn against a hardening conscience. "We live today," says Dr. Robert E. Fitch in *Christianity and Crisis,* "in an age when ethics is becoming obsolete. It is superseded by science, deleted by psychology, dismissed as emotive by philosophy: it is drowned in compassion, evaporates into aesthetics and retreats before relativism. . . . The usual moral distinctions are simply drowned in a maudlin emotion in which we have more feeling for the murderer than for the murdered, for the adulterer than for the betrayed; and in which we gradually begin to believe that the really guilty party, the one who somehow caused it all, is the victim, not the perpetrator, of the crime."

America is said to have the highest per capita boredom of any spot on earth. We have tried to fill ourselves with science and education, with better living and pleasure, with the many other things we thought we wanted, but we are still empty and bored. Why are we empty? Because the Creator made us for Himself, and we shall never find completeness and fulness apart from fellowship with Him. Jesus told us long ago that "man shall not live by bread alone," but we have paid no heed. We have gone on stuffing ourselves with bread of every description—except the bread Christ offered. We are desperately weary of the emptiness and boredom within. We are confused by the prejudice, hatred, greed and lust that are within us. We seem to be caught in quicksand: we want out of our human dilemma but are powerless. The American genius has enabled us to change everything but ourselves.

It is absolutely impossible to change society and reverse the moral trend unless we ourselves are changed from the inside out. Man needs transformation or conversion. Unless we Americans are willing to humbly accept the diagnosis of the Book upon which our culture was largely founded—

and to accept its remedy—we are going to continue along the road to disaster and ruin. No nation in history has had a greater opportunity than America. Because our privileges have been greater, our responsibilities are greater. Thus, a Holy God requires more of the American people than of any nation in the history of the world with the possible exception of Israel. Our only way to moral reform is through repentance of our sins and a return to God.

Confronted with the evidences of spiritual and moral decay on every hand, we now find ourselves more frequently looking for relief from the consequences of our waywardness rather than to the cause and cure of the desperate situation in which we find ourselves. In the Old Testament we read, "If my people, which are called by my name, shall humble themselves, and pray, and seek my face, and turn from their wicked ways; then will I hear from heaven, and will forgive their sin, and will heal their land." Here is a formula of God's own making, a way by which a nation may return to a right relationship with Him. But I repeat, it is men who must be changed before a nation can be changed.

I am not so naive as to believe that all personal and national problems would be solved if all men should have this transformation. But in Christ the personal problem of sin, which is the "root cause" of many of our problems, would be answered. A new atmosphere could be created as we approach the complicated social and political problems of our corporate life. We would then have the inner strength, courage and ability to cope with these problems. America can rise no higher than the individuals who walk her streets, conduct her business, teach her young people, make her homes and attend her churches. It is these individuals who must be changed. As compelling as are the great social needs of our nation and of the world, these can only be met as individuals are themselves. It was to make new men and women that Christ came into the world.

VI

Can We Count on More Dedicated People?

JOHN W. GARDNER

CRITICS ARE SAYING THAT WE HAVE LOST OUR DEVOTION TO American ideals. They are saying that the individual American has lost his faith, his discipline and his vitality. They are saying that he is a spoiled, demanding, overfed oaf who cares for nothing but his own creature comforts and diversion.

I don't believe it.

But something is wrong. At a moment in our history when we need all our sense of purpose and capacity for sustained effort, we seem in danger of losing our bearings, of surrendering to a "cult of easiness."

Why? Others have tried to explain our failures at the level of national policy and leadership. Such explanations are undoubtedly helpful. It is my intention, however, to explore the question as it touches the citizen.

Our national problems have become so complex that it is not easy for the individual to see what he can do about them. The tasks facing the frontiersmen two centuries ago may have been grim, but they were also obvious. Each man knew what he must do. But what can a man of today do about inflation, about international organization, about the balance of trade? There are answers to these questions, but they are not self-evident. The individual American—busy earning a living, repapering the dining room, getting the children off to school, paying the bills—doesn't hear one clear call to action. He hears a jumble of outcries and alarms, of fanfares and dirges, of voices crying "Hurry!" and voices crying "Wait!" Meanwhile he has problems of his own.

The men who founded this nation knew that in a world largely hostile to the idea of freedom, a free society would have to prove that it is capable of, and worthy of, survival. The requirement is unchanged today. Free societies must prove their ability to make good on their promises and to keep alive their cherished values. And they must prove their vigor, their capacity to practice the disciplined virtues. Above all, they must prove their capacity to achieve excellence.

The free society is still the exceptional society, and the world is still full of people who believe that men need masters. The survival of the idea for which this nation stands is not inevitable. It may survive if enough Americans care enough.

It would be easier to grasp that truth if we weren't so blessedly comfortable. Part of our problem is how to stay awake on a full stomach. Since the beginning of time most humans have had to work hard either because subsistence demanded it or because their taskmasters required it. Now we don't have to work very hard to stay alive; and free people have no taskmasters. With such release from outward pressures, free men may make the fatal mistake of thinking that no effort is required of them.

Nothing could be more dangerous to our future. Free men must be quick to understand the kinds of effort that are required to keep their society vital and strong. If they have the wisdom to demand much of themselves, their society will flourish. But a free society that refuses to exert itself will not last long. And freedom alone won't save it.

Americans have many differing ideas about the appropriate goals for our society. That is as it should be. But we do have shared aims. And our hope of greatness as a nation lies in these shared aims. No people in history ever lifted itself above the normal trajectory without a widely shared "vision of greatness."

Some people say that we are uncertain of our shared aims. Some say we're drifting because we've achieved everything we ever wanted. Both statements are dead wrong. To say that we are confused is one way of evading the difficult tasks before us. We are not really in doubt about the more serious of our shared aims. We know what they are. We know that they are difficult. And we know that we have not achieved them.

Are examples needed?

We want peace with justice. We want a world that doesn't live under the fear of the bomb, a world that acknowledges the rule of law, a world in which no nation can play bully and no nation need live in fear. How many

Americans would disagree with that purpose? Is it easy? Have we come close to achieving it? Read your morning paper.

We want freedom. We don't think man was born to have someone else's foot on his neck—or someone else's hand over his mouth. We want freedom at home and we want a world in which freedom is possible. Who would disagree with that as a national aim? Who would call it easy? Who would say we've achieved it?

We believe in the dignity and worth of the individual, and it has always been our unshakable purpose to protect and preserve that dignity.

We believe that every person should be enabled to achieve the best that is in him, and we are the declared enemies of disease, ignorance, poverty and all other conditions which stunt the individual and prevent such fulfillment.

We believe in equality before the law, in equal political suffrage, and—dearest of all to Americans—equality of opportunity. "We may not all hit home runs," the saying goes, "but every man should have his chance at bat."

Those are only some of the more obvious goals we are committed to as Americans. Have we gone as far as we should in achieving them? Are all our problems solved? Look around.

In the world at large we see the threat of universal destruction. We see great nations striving fiercely to prove that free societies are outmoded. We see underdeveloped lands stirring out of their ancient sleep, poised between chaos and orderly development, listening indiscriminately to those who would help them and those who would use them.

At home we see—despite our impressive achievements in

human welfare—still too many children trapped in poverty and ignorance; too many talents blighted by lack of opportunity; too many men and women who never achieve their full potential; racial and religious prejudice in the South and in the North; the invasion of personal freedom by government and by large organizations; juvenile delinquency and social disintegration in the big cities; corruption and the misuse of power; and creeping mediocrity in every phase of our national life.

Is this a fair picture of our nation? Of course not. Our achievements in providing a better life for Americans are astounding to other societies. We may be deeply proud of what we've accomplished. But smugness and complacency do not look good on us. Our historic attitude has been pride in what we've accomplished and impatience that we haven't accomplished more. Let's not change now.

Obviously we don't agree on how to deal with our major problems. As free Americans we will argue that question right to the door of the polling booth.

But we know what the problems are and agree on our more important aims. So what is lacking? The answer is simple: We lack leadership on the part of our leaders, and commitment on the part of every American. I want to talk about the matter of individual "commitment."

The establishment of a durable peace, the strengthening of a free society, the enrichment of the traditions on which freedom depends—these cannot be achieved by aimless or listless men. All our wisdom, all our talent and vitality, all our steadfastness will be needed if we wish to attain these goals. Can we count on an ample supply of dedicated Americans?

The answer must be conditional. If—as a nation—we

understand, expect and honor dedication, the supply will be ample. But if we assume that dedicated men are exceedingly rare and probably a little foolish, the supply will be low. It is unfortunately true that Americans have to some degree lost the habit of asking for or expecting devoted action. Long continued, such failure to expect dedication can have only one outcome: we shall eventually lose the capacity for it.

Of course every line of behavior has its pathology, and there is a pathology of dedication. People sometimes commit themselves to vicious or criminal goals. Or their commitment to worthy goals becomes so fanatical that they destroy as much as they create. And there is the "true believer" who surrenders himself to a mass movement or to dogmatic beliefs in order to escape the responsibilities of freedom. A free society does not invite that kind of allegiance. It wants only one kind of devotion—the devotion of free, rational, responsible individuals.

It is my conviction that free and responsible individuals are proud to offer such devotion if given the opportunity. People would rather work hard for something they believe in than enjoy a pampered idleness. They would rather sacrifice their comfort for an honored objective than pursue endless diversions. It is a mistake to speak of dedication as a sacrifice. Every man knows that there is exhilaration in intense effort applied toward a meaningful end. The religious precept that you must lose yourself to find yourself is no less true at the secular level. No one who has observed the devoted scientist in his laboratory can doubt the spiritual rewards of such work. The same is true of anyone who is working toward goals that represent the highest values of his society.

We fall into the error of thinking that happiness necessarily involves ease, diversion, tranquillity—a state in which all of one's wishes are satisfied. For most people happiness is not to be found in this vegetative state but in striving toward meaningful goals. The dedicated person has not achieved all of his goals. His life is the endless pursuit of goals, some of them unattainable. He may never have time to surround himself with luxuries. He may often be tense, worried, fatigued. He has little of the leisure one associates with the storybook conception of happiness.

But he has found a more meaningful happiness. The truth is that happiness in the sense of total gratification is not a state to which man can aspire. It is for the cows, possibly for the birds, but not for us.

We want meaning in our lives. When we raise our sights, strive for excellence and dedicate ourselves to the highest goals of our society, we are enrolling in an ancient and meaningful cause: the age-long struggle of man to realize the best that is in him. Man reaching toward the most exalted goals he can conceive, man striving impatiently and restlessly for excellence has produced great religious insights, created great art, penetrated secrets of the universe and set standards of conduct which give meaning to the phrase "the dignity of man." On the other hand, man without standards, man with his eyes on the ground has proven over and over, in every society, at every period in history, that humans can be lower than the beasts, sunk in ignorance, morally and ethically blind, living a life devoid of meaning.

The task we face as a nation of keeping our ideals alive is partly a question of leadership. Even in a democracy leaders must lead. If our citizens are to recapture a sense of mission with respect to the purposes we care the most about, our leaders must have the capacity and the vision to ask for it. It is hard to expect an upsurge of devotion to the common good in response to leaders who lack the moral depth to understand such devotion—or the courage to evoke it, or the stature to merit the response which follows. One of the great tasks of leadership is to help a society achieve the best that is in it.

But it takes more than leadership to preserve the ideals of a free society. The values we cherish will not survive without the constant attention of the ordinary citizen. Unlike the Pyramids, the monuments of the spirit will not stand untended. They must be nourished in each generation by the allegiance of believing men and women. The fact that millions have died violent deaths while defending individual freedom does not ensure survival of that principle if we cease paying our tithes of devotion. Every free man, in his work and in his family life, in his public behavior and in the secret places of his heart, should see himself as a builder and maintainer of the ideals of his society. Individual Americans—truck drivers and editors, grocers and senators, beauty operators and ballplayers—can contribute to the greatness and strength of a free society, or they can help it to die.

How does one contribute to the greatness and strength of a free society? That is a question to which there are many true answers. One answer is—pursue excellence! Those who are most devoted to a democratic society must be precisely the ones who insist that free men are capable of the highest standards of performance, that a free society can be a great society in the richest sense of that phrase. The idea for which this nation stands will not survive if the highest goal free men can set themselves is an amiable mediocrity.

At the simplest level, the pursuit of excellence means an increased concern for competence on the part of the individual. Keeping a free society free—and vital and strong—is no job for the half-educated and the slovenly. In a society of free men competence is a primary duty. The man who does his job well tones up the whole society. And the man who does a slovenly job—whether he is a janitor or a judge, a surgeon or a technician—lowers the tone of the society. So do the chiselers of high and low degree, the sleight-of-hand artists who know how to gain an advantage without honest work. They are the regrettable burdens of a free society.

But excellence implies more than competence. It implies a striving for the highest standards in every phase of life. We need individual excellence in all its forms, in every kind of creative endeavor, in political life, in education, in industry—in short, universally. And, not least, we need excellence in standards of individual conduct.

The words for Americans to live by are these: If you believe in a free society, be worthy of a free society. You don't need to quit your job and enroll as a missionary in Africa to prove your dedication. Stay where you are and do a better job, be a better citizen, live a better life. Every good man strengthens society. In this day of sophisticated judgments on man and society, that is a notably unfashionable thing to say, but it is true. Men of integrity, by their very existence, rekindle the belief that as a people we can live above the level of moral squalor. We need that belief, for a cynical community is a corrupt community. More than any other form of government, democracy requires a certain optimism concerning mankind. The best argument for democracy is the existence of men who justify that optimism. It follows that one of the best ways to serve democracy is to be that kind of man. When you see such men and women, tip your hat and bow. The future of our civilization is in their hands.

VII

We Must Show the Way to Enduring Peace

Clinton Rossiter

THE UNITED STATES IS RIGHTLY NUMBERED AMONG THOSE nations for which a benevolent sense of national purpose —or, as I prefer, of mission—has been a historical necessity. We have been, like the children of Israel, a "peculiar treasure." Upon us destiny has bestowed special favor; of us it has therefore asked special effort. Because men like Washington and Lincoln sensed this grand truth and acted consciously upon it, we have counted more heavily in history than our size and wealth, however majestic, would seem to have warranted. The world, we must think, would be in a far different and unhappier situation today if there had never been a United States.

If we think that, we must also think that it will be in a

far different and unhappier situation in 25 or 50 or 100 years unless the United States survives and flourishes. We are, however, besieged with doubts about our capacity to flourish and perhaps even to survive. The sharpest doubt of all is compounded of two related suspicions: that we have lost the sense of mission of our early years, and yet that we need this sense more desperately than ever today.

We need it because we stand at one of those rare points in history when a nation must choose consciously between greatness and mediocrity. The United States may well go on for centuries as a territorial entity in which men and women can pursue reasonably useful and satisfying lives. Will it also be, as it has hitherto been, a unique civilization whose decline would be counted a major calamity in history? That is the choice we must now make. If we choose greatness, as surely we must, we choose effort—the kind of national effort that transcends the ordinary lives of men and commits them to the pursuit of a common purpose, that persuades them to sacrifice private indulgences to the public interest, that sends them on a search for leaders who call forth strengths rather than pander to weaknesses.

Such an effort must have its beginning in the minds and hearts of Americans, and take the form of a clear statement of the meaning and goals of a unique people. America will not flourish, not in the hot winds of this volcanic age, unless it can develop a profound, inspiring, benevolent sense of mission. While this is only the first short step to the grandeur to which we may still properly aspire, it is the kind that must be taken boldly before any other can be attempted.

One reason why we must take it boldly, or not bother to take it at all, is that it will not be easy. As an historian, I am bound to point out that this country stands on shaky historical and cultural ground from which to launch a new search for a national mission and then to pursue it. The sense of mission seems to spring most readily from the consciousness of a young nation, even of a nation in the making, and America, alas, is well into middle age.

In our youth we had a profound sense of national purpose, which we lost over the years of our rise to glory. The American mission that inspired every statesman from Washington through Lincoln called upon us to serve as a testament to freedom, to spread by our example the good news of personal liberty and popular government throughout the world. We did not lose our youthful sense of mission because it was childish or wicked or impossible in its demands upon us, rather because it had to be fulfilled in the course of time or be cast aside as a youthful extravagance. And it was in fact fulfilled nobly. For all its areas of blighted hope, the world today counts many constitutional democracies where once it counted only the United States.

Can a nation that has fulfilled the mission of its youth expect to find a second mission in its later years? And can a nation that has known the material success of ours shake loose from the clutch of self-indulgence? Once we were lean and hungry, a people "on the make," and we generated a sense of mission almost instinctively in order to survive and move ahead. Now we are fat and complacent, a people that "has it made," and we find it hard to rouse to the trumpet of sacrifice—even if anyone in authority were to blow it.

Still another hurdle in the path of our search for a new sense of national purpose is the cherished doctrine of American individualism, which has taught even the most dependent of us to look with suspicion on the community and its demands. The characteristic American, if such a man there be, is too much an individualist to listen comfortably to men who talk of a collective destiny. Out of the lives of millions of free, decent, duty-conscious individuals there may well arise, this American thinks, some greater purpose: progress for the human race, glory for God, the triumph of liberty. Yet essentially he is a man who, try as he might, can find no ultimate purpose in history that justifies an exaltation of the nation, no cosmic plan for America that gives special meaning to his life and thus calls for special sacrifice.

Finally, we are faced with the hard question: Who speaks for America? Who can state our mission in such a way that, if truthfully and eloquently stated, it will be accepted and acted upon by the American people? We have no Marx, no teacher revered as the First Source. We have no Pope, no God-touched prophet whose words command unique respect. To redirect the aspirations of an entire people is a monstrous task, especially if the people has always been encouraged to speak in a confusion of tongues and to listen with suspicion to the voices of its leaders. The machinery of freedom is not effectively geared to produce and disseminate the One Big Idea, even if it be the idea of freedom. If this country is ever to recapture a sense of national purpose, that purpose will have to be voiced by a line of plain-talking presidents and given a cutting edge in laws enacted by a series of tough-minded congresses. Then it will have to be put into daily practice by tens of thousands of dedicated administrators, teachers, ministers, editors, managers and community leaders.

These are genuine difficulties, yet they need not prove

insuperable, certainly not for a nation with the untapped resolve that ours still carries within it; and, in any case we are bound by every imperative of tradition, patriotism and morality to make the attempt. Where, then, are we to find this idea, this new sense of national purpose, and what form are we to give it? The answer, I submit, lies waiting for discovery in the history and present condition of the American people.

The history is one of genuine achievement. Our failures have been shocking, but our triumphs have been earth-shaking. To have occupied a continent, created a new nation out of the surplus of other nations, built up a giant society based on individual liberty, maintained an effective government based on popular consent, led all nations in producing and distributing the fruits of technology, given unique dignity and fulfillment to the lives of ordinary men, and stood before the world as an example of the blessings of freedom are achievements of which we might well be more conscious and proud. Surely a nation that has just come from doing such deeds should be able to do others no less historic. Surely such a nation has no choice but to do them—or cease to be the nation it has always been.

The present condition, plainly, is one of growing un-easiness. We are sliding into a series of discontents to whose solution the energies of a consciously dedicated people may alone be equal. While I do not wish to sound too presumptuous or pat in my catalogue of these discontents, I can best describe the crisis of our age as a tangle of four separate yet curiously related crises: the crisis in race relations, the crisis in culture, the crisis of the community, and the crisis of peace and war—all of which are growing in intensity with each passing year.

The crisis in the relations of the white majority and the Negro minority in this country is the oldest, most puzzling and most distressing with which we have ever been faced or may ever be. This situation is especially puzzling because of our contrasting success in dealing with many problems in the area of social relations that have been the despair and even the destruction of other societies. We took the lead in softening the impact of religious differences upon the delicate pattern of social harmony; we have made a mockery of Marx's insistence upon the universality of the class struggle; we have converted mobility from a threat to social stability into one of its stoutest supports. Yet always we have known that every claim for the fairness of our social order had to be footnoted "except for the Negroes."

If we can say anything for certain about American society in 1960, it is that the Negroes are no longer a footnote and we can no longer make them an exception. They are a powerful presence, 18 million Americans growing daily less content with the status and symbols of third-class citizenship, 18 million Americans with determined, conscience-stricken allies in the white majority. We must take it as a fact of history that we will have no peace in our minds nor self-esteem in our hearts until we have broadened the boundaries of American democracy to include the Negro (and, I might add, the Puerto Rican, Indian and the Asian), until we have built a system in which equal justice, equal respect and equal opportunity are the patrimony of all Americans.

The crisis in American culture is perhaps more obvious to the schoolteacher than to the housewife, to the artist than to the salesman, to the egghead than to the hardhead. It is a crisis nonetheless, for surely no great nation can be said to be worth respecting or imitating if it has not achieved a high level of culture, and it is at least an arguable question whether this nation will ever achieve it.

I do not mean to ignore our genuine successes in the many fields of art and learning, nor to disparage those Americans who have won them for us. If we are not Athenians or Florentines, neither are we Philistines. Yet we lack a widespread popular respect for the fruits of art and learning and for those who produce them, and we have much too short a supply of first-class artists and intellectuals. More than that, no people in history has ever had to put up with so much vulgarity, cheapness and ugliness in its surroundings. History has flung us an exciting challenge by making us the first of all nations in which men of every rank could display a measure of taste; we have responded by displaying bad taste on a massive scale—and by exporting some of the worst examples of this taste to countries all over the world. Let us be honest about it: we have the wealth and leisure and techniques to make a great culture an essential part of our lives, an inspiration to the world, and a monument for future generations—and we have not even come close to the mark. When will we come to realize that lives without culture are lives only half lived, that the arts can be introduced in a hundred subtle ways to enrich our daily comings and goings, and that there is no pride to match that of living in a country that is taken seriously by the world as a fountain of art and letters?

The crisis of the community is one that has burst upon us only in the past few years. I mean, of course, the steadily widening gap between the richness of our private lives and the poverty of our public services, between a standard of living inside our homes that is the highest in the world and a standard of living outside them that is fast becoming a national disgrace. The American economy is wonderfully constructed, technically and ideologically, to satisfy the demands of a rapidly growing population for food, clothing, entertainment, private transportation, labor-saving devices, luxuries and much of its housing. It is only poorly constructed to do what so plainly needs to be done about the blight of our cities, the shortage of water and power, the disappearance of open space, the inadequacy of education, the need for recreational facilities, the high incidence of crime and delinquency, the crowding of the roads, the decay of the railroads, the ugliness of the sullied landscape, the pollution of the very air we breathe.

These public problems will never be handled in the style of a great nation until we rid our minds of threadbare prejudices about the role of government, value the things we buy with our taxes as highly as those we buy with what is left over after taxes, and distribute our richest treasure—men and women of intelligence and character—more judiciously among the callings and professions. We lure far too many talented young people into advertising and far too few into city planning, far too many into car-dealing and far too few into teaching, far too many into high-priced private psychiatry and far too few into low-cost public health. The gross misuse of human resources is a situation that cries out for correction.

Looming above and aggravating all our other crises is the desperate situation of a world one-third uncertainly free, one-third aggressively totalitarian, one-third racked by poverty, hunger, envy and the pangs of awakening nationalism. The first two of these mighty camps are so awesomely armed that they could destroy one another as going civilizations in a matter of hours. Around their peripheries we find points of frightening volatility, any one of them capable of triggering a war that would put an abrupt end to all speculations about the higher destiny of the American people.

Even if we can forestall the crisis of a war that will be worse than war, we are left deep in the crisis of a peace that is no peace. We pour an appalling amount of money, resources, skills and energy into the development and production of weapons we pray to God we will never use. I am aware that much of the waste is imperative, that the menace of the Soviet Union has left us only a small range of choice in deciding how much of our total resources we should spend on national defense. I can, however, draw little comfort from the thought that we have done merely our duty to ourselves and to our allies. Sitting on the edge of an abyss costs a great deal in spiritual as well as material resources.

These are not the only major troubles that are plaguing this country today, but no other current problem, not even the much discussed crisis in morals, presents so urgent a challenge to a nation that has been great, remains great, and must now choose consciously whether it will be great in the future. These four problems are the unfinished business of American democracy; they are the tests of our determination to remain a notable civilization; they are the raw materials out of which we will spin the sense of national purpose we need so badly.

It is, I think, the last of these problems that presents this nation with its most fateful challenge to greatness. In the crisis of war and peace—in the yearning of mankind to be done with wars and rumors of wars and to build up the conditions of a secure and bountiful peace—we will find, if we are ever to find it at all, a renewed sense of national purpose, a second American mission. Several considerations make this choice as appealing as it is inevitable.

First, the challenge of peace looms above the others in present urgency and future import. No purpose of the American people could be more pressing than that of forestalling a savage war that all participants and spectators are certain to lose. The achievement of this purpose would give us first rank among all nations in the histories of the future; the refusal to conceive and act upon it would expose us to ridicule and shame. We brought ourselves, virtually unaided to the center of the stage of history, and we will fail all mankind as well as ourselves if we do not act greatly upon it.

Second, this challenge seems much the best calculated to unite the American people. The unity of the nation in the face of vast centrifugal forces has been one of its most treasured possessions, and we are bound to consider it carefully as we make our historic choice of a second American mission. No other problem directs itself so immediately to every American; no other calls for sacrifices from every man and woman in due proportion; no other holds out a richer reward to every group and interest and section.

This is by no means to downgrade the vast benefits to be gained for the health and reputation of the United States in a forceful, imaginative pursuit of the other goals I have indicated. Indeed, we must pursue them steadily at peril of breaking faith with our historic commitment to liberty, justice, opportunity and well-being. Yet they are also goals that may be reached more quickly by a nation committed to leadership in the search for enduring peace. Although history and circumstance both support our claim to such leadership, the claim will remain suspect to most nations of the world so long as we punish men of color for claiming the rights of other Americans, make trash our major cultural export, and starve the efforts of the community to serve our public needs. The search for peace incorporates, strengthens and transcends the search for equity in race relations, quality in culture and balance in the political economy. All these searches must go forward together.

Finally, the challenge of peace calls upon us to deal not just with ourselves but with all mankind, and thus throws our self-awareness as a nation into sharpest focus. A sense of national purpose is at bottom a sense of international purpose, whether evil or benevolent in its influence upon the rest of the world. In the absence of any desire to influence the world, or even to do business with it, the quest for a sense of national purpose becomes an exercise in futility.

How then are we to frame our response as a nation to this greatest of challenges? What are we to consider our special role in the search of all nations for a peace that rewards them with freedom, security, justice and opportunity? The answer, once again, stares us patiently in the face. To find it we need only look with fresh eyes at the poignant situation of a rich, proud and successful nation in a world full of poor, bewildered and aspiring nations.

All things considered, especially the psychological and ideological distance we had to travel from the aloofness of 1938 to the involvement of 1948, we have done remarkably well in honoring our obligations to this world. We have helped to keep the peace, we have spread our bounty widely. Yet the peace is fragile and costly, the bounty has made only a small dent in the sufferings of mankind. The time has surely come for a new American approach to the world outside. While the immediate pressure to adopt a new approach may result from the ubiquitous activities of the Soviet Union, the next great step to a peaceful world would seem, in any case, to be the special responsibility of the United States.

In my opinion, it has now become the destiny of this nation to lead the world prudently and pragmatically—step by step, pact by pact, concession by concession—through cooperation to confederacy to federation and at last to a government having power to enforce peace. There is little doubt that the world is moving fitfully in this direction, and the mightiest nation should show the way rather than drag its feet. This, surely, is the second American mission. While the process may and should take several generations—and may need a few small catastrophes to spur it onward—the ultimate goal and our responsibility for leading the way toward it must never be lost from sight. In the next century the world will achieve a peace of abundance and justice through law or become a vast basket of crabs in which the struggle for bare survival consumes the energies of all nations.

The second American mission will not be easy for us to go on, for we will have to redirect some of our deepest urges toward ends that our fathers would have found unthinkable. It will not be easy for us to complete, for we cannot be sure that mankind, even under the most prudent leadership and with the best of luck, will be spared the agonies of nuclear war. The fact that it calls for new ways of thinking and for calculated risks is, however, no reason not to enter upon it boldly.

Let us labor, then, in the world at large—in the United Nations, in the World Court, in conferences at Geneva, in the reach into space, in the dozen great ventures in which we have already begun to surrender some aspect of our pristine sovereignty—with this lofty purpose in mind. While we keep our defenses up, let us look with fresh eyes for ways to tear them down. While we pursue our present program of foreign aid, let us consider whether we are not in fact stingy to the point of absurdity. While we use force when force is the only workable means, let us remember that true leadership is largely an exercise in example and persuasion. We are called upon by history to guide the world, not to dominate it. And while we continue to cherish the fond belief that our country is a peculiar treasure, let us perceive that it is just such a country that may rise above its apparent self-interest in a grand attempt to secure the interest of humanity. To make such an attempt we must, like Jefferson and his colleagues, be aware that we are acting "not for ourselves alone, but for the whole human race."

A nation that has counted as a special force in history must strive to count again or reap the fruits of demoralization. Having once been great, we cannot endure to be mediocre. Like tens of millions of Americans, I live in grateful awareness of our past achievements. Like perhaps a few million less, I want to die—well, a half-century from now—knowing that we had gone on to even greater achievements. Above all, I want to die—and shouldn't all Americans?—suspecting that this country would be remembered and saluted down through the centuries for its services to "the whole human race."

VIII

No Highway to High Purpose

ALBERT WOHLSTETTER

WHEN WE ASK OURSELVES WHAT HAS HAPPENED TO OUR
national purpose, we sound vaguely as if, in a moment of
absent-mindedness, we had mislaid it. In fact, our first
self-conscious impulse is to see where we may have left it.
Shall we look in the Constitution? Will we perhaps find it
in something Lincoln or Woodrow Wilson said? What our
Founding Fathers have said remains important and inspiring. Still, neglect of their teachings cannot be the whole
story, for in the last decade or so, while our purpose is said
to have been ebbing, their teachings have been less neg-
lected than in preceding times.

Nonetheless, if the nationwide questioning of national
purpose evokes uneasy stirrings, it is for this very reason
useful. It indicates that we are in trouble, that a further
questioning and debate are in order. But the limitation of

the questions raised so far is that they ask for very general
answers, for a statement of ends without any explicit weigh-
ing of means or costs. They sometimes seem to imply,
therefore, that our difficulties are not really complex, deep
or particular, and that they can be solved by a simple
reaffirmation—and of some one thing at that. To ask for
our national purpose suggests that there is one high over-
riding aim waiting ready-made, if not to be found by leaf-
ing through some documents, perhaps to be revealed effort-
lessly as in a dream, "the American dream." Even the word
"mission," frequently used in discussions of national purpose, connotes revealed truth rather than working programs to be won by hard analysis of what we want and
what we can do and the efforts needed. While we may talk
about national purpose in the singular, the first thing to
observe about our aims is that we have many of them. They
are connected; some depend on others; many conflict. Obviously two aims may conflict when each represents the interests of a different group. But even ends which the nation
as a whole can be said to share oppose other accepted
national ends.

Take "the common defense"—a purpose of nationhood
recognized by the Founding Fathers, and even more critical today. We all want to avoid getting killed in a missile
raid. On the other hand, most of us would like to see an
increase in our present enjoyments. Yet reducing the
chance of our demolition is at odds with getting the utmost
in production of civilian goods and services. Deciding to
reduce the risk that we may have no future at all is only
an extreme form of the choice between present and future
enjoyments—a choice we make in the everyday act of saving

—and there is a growing public recognition of the importance of that choice.

There are other conflicts. We want to make the new nations of the world more stable and help them abolish poverty by technical innovation—but innovation means change and instability. We would like to increase democracy everywhere, but this conflicts with our desire not to interfere with the internal affairs of other nations. We hope to propagate the peaceable uses of science and technology, but in doing so we spread information about methods of destruction. We want to defend the independent non-Communist countries but this increases the hostility of the Communist world. In all these matters our desires are complex and partially conflicting.

To make fundamental choices, we must understand specific means as well as general ends. Today we need to learn about intricate and uncertain matters, like missiles and their implications. We must contemplate some extremely unpleasant possibilities, just because we want to avoid them and achieve something better. Nobody, however, likes to think about anything unpleasant, even to avoid it. And so the crucial problem of thermonuclear war is frequently dispatched with the label "War is unthinkable"— which, translated freely, means we don't want to think about it. But a purpose hammered out of connected and partially conflicting desires has to be the product of reflection and choice, and if the problems are profound the choice, once made, calls for exertion. There is, unfortunately, no highway leading to high purpose.

We cannot resolve the conflict of ends by the simple device of choosing *one* and ignoring all the others. This is true even of such important ends as reducing the risk of annihilation, a fact which explains the almost universal disparagement of "mere survival" as a national goal. We want much more than simply to survive. To preserve and extend democracy inside our own boundaries and in other parts of the world is not just a nice thought; it is vital. If we did not take these goals seriously, physical survival might be easy. We could reduce the danger of thermo-nuclear attack on the United States by giving the Com-munists free anything they might want to take by aggres-sion. In fact, several eminent non-Communist Englishmen have suggested this alternative for our consideration. In rejecting it, however, we need not sound excessively dis-dainful about the value of keeping alive. Physical survival is necessary to achieve our other widely shared purposes, even though it is not enough.

When we have tended in the past to fix on one goal to the exclusion of others, we have in effect been evading the responsibility for taking greater pains. Since World War II our policy has been notable for both an extreme reluctance to call for national effort and a wild oscillation from one purpose to another, rather than a steady stress on some combination of goals.

For example, we have gone from supporting emergency economic aid for our allies to concentrating on their de-fense so exclusively that most economic aid had to be repre-sented as "defense support." We have swung from uni-lateral disarmament—and a neglect of the Communist threat —to rearmament and even to a conception that negotiations with the Communists are futile, if not treasonable, and that liberation of the satellites should come first. In recoil from this extreme and out of sheer fatigue, many of us have stalked enormous hopes on the possibility of concluding broad agreements with the Russians soon, and our resolution to defend parts of the free world against Communist aggression has become subject to doubt. Now the ghost of Paris has displaced the Spirit of Camp David and the Spirit of Geneva, and we may fear another emotional swing.

Throughout all these swings since the war, our wish for cheap answers concealed from us the depth of our problems. We adopted a technical assistance program as an inexpensive substitute for American capital to develop backward countries. A defense of our allies was based on nuclear threat rather than on matching the non-nuclear forces of our antagonists. Collections of gadgetry were hopefully supposed to provide a defense of our cities at modest cost. And now there has been a stripping of our air defense and a search undertaken for a method of deterring war with a minimum of effort and a maximum of hope. For some, negotiations with the Russians were a labor-saving gadget to achieve stability at even lower defense levels. But the tremendous political and technical revolutions that rack the world today exclude any cheap or single solution. We may fear that our achievements are menaced by the need to make an effort. I think this is wrong. They are threatened by the risks involved in failing to make an effort.

We have deep troubles, crises that call for resolution and leadership. It is worth saying, however, especially since laments about the "quality of American life" have become a ritual, that there are very large areas in our society which do not call for leadership and common purposes.

There may indeed be a crisis in American culture, as some of the contributors to this debate believe. I am not sure. Myself, I don't care for tail fins or Elvis or advertising jingles or even Coca-Cola, but I doubt that their popularity is a national danger. An immense sea of mediocrity surrounds but has not submerged poets such as Robert Lowell and Elizabeth Bishop, artists of the order of Alexander Calder, the choreographers Martha Graham and George Balanchine, and an abundance of excellent architects—Mies van der Rohe, Eero Saarinen, Gorden Bunshafte, Marcel Breuer, Walter Gropius, Richard Neutra and many others. New York concert halls offer an extraordinary range of music from ancient to modern that is unmatched in Paris, London or Rome. The audience for the best in art, music and literature may be limited, but so far it always has been, and I am more impressed than some with the wide accessibility of great works made possible by the long-playing record and the paperback. Perhaps, as Pablo Casals has said, when good music is easy to hear it can successfully compete with rock 'n' roll.

However, if it cannot, I doubt that anything our leaders have to say will help much. Whatever their differences on domestic and foreign policy, Mr. Truman's and Mr. Eisenhower's comments on contemporary art are similarly unflattering and would lead us nowhere I want to go. In any case I don't think we should all be going to the same place. In the area of our private enjoyments we can dispense with a single voice speaking for America.

There are, however, critical points at which private aims become a public concern. For example, as individuals we decide where to live, where to work, and how to travel to and from work; but if multiplied a millionfold without public guidance these decisions are not likely to be compatible at all. In fact they have brought about intolerable congestion and an urban sprawl desired by no one. Again, we are being forced to recognize that even individual decisions about where to eat or whom to serve in restaurants or to transport in buses are an urgent common concern. Clearly we must put high on our agenda a large extension of freedom and equality of opportunity especially to American minorities: the Negro, the Puerto Rican, the Indian and the Asian. Such a domestic purpose is worthy in its own right, and it also bears an obvious relation to our foreign policy. Race prejudice at home is an enormous handicap to any nation aspiring to lead a non-Communist world that is largely colored.

And foreign policy plays an increasingly important role in the American political scene. Most Americans seem to agree on the need for foreign economic and military aid. The growing recognition that our national ends must be international in scope is a sign of increasing national maturity. To disperse the benefits of technology, to expand the forces of production so as to end poverty, and at the same time to extend political freedom and self-government in the world—these are great aspirations. As aspirations, they appear in the United Nations charter, which was signed without embarrassment by some of freedom's sworn enemies. To bring them down from the level of pious benevolence to something concrete enough to deserve the name of purpose requires the evolution of detailed and consistent policies. And we face enormous problems in assisting the non-Communist countries in their economic and political self-development, if at the same time we want to help them to remain free of Communist domination.

For a candid look at the "free world" suggests that the phrase, if not a euphemism, has a circumscribed meaning. It means "free from the domination of the Communist bloc" and covers nations with a tremendous variety of political institutions, ranging from those few that have an effective multiparty system and a considerable popular control to a very large number of authoritarian regimes. The truth is that in the world today there are only a few local enclaves of representative democracy.

In much of Latin America, more than a century after liberation from Spain and Portugal, dictatorships succeed one another and representative government, though symbolized in many constitutions, is an unrealized ideal. And colonialism in Africa and Asia prepared its subjects no better for democratic self-rule. While the technological revolutions under way will bring tremendous changes, few nations have institutions that permit internal shifts in political power without violence, and the time when such institutions will be general is a long way off. Even more remote is a world government ensuring that revolutionary shifts in power among nations can take place without violence.

Today many influential people believe that disarmament is the shortest path to world government as well as the only hope of avoiding a world-wide nuclear war. I believe that arms control may achieve very useful ends, but only if its limitations are understood. No arms agreement in prospect will bring us within shouting distance of world government. And while some agreed arrangements might add a little more stability to our present uneasy peace, others could make the balance even more precarious.

An examination of some of the great and complex issues of war, peace, and arms control will show why defining national purposes will take much hard thought and produce no panacea. We tend emotionally to associate peace

and all that is good with treaties and international arrangements, just as we associate war and all that is bad with
arms. But our emotions mislead us in these simple equa-
tions. The principal goal of American arms today is to
avoid war by deterring aggression. And history is replete
with international agreements which have actually encouraged aggression.

Still it would be unfortunate if, reacting from our excessive wishfulness before the recent Summit meeting, we
now considered realistic agreements neither possible nor
useful. For agreements might slow the increase or dispersion of a military technology that favored aggression
rather than defense. They might limit the size of various
military forces, or their method and area of operation, or
provide information as to their whereabouts. By such devices agreements might lower the likelihood of war being
started deliberately or as the result of an "accident" or
misunderstanding. They could reduce aggressive capabilities or provide warning of an actual aggression or reassur-
ance that no aggression is under way, and so make mutual
deterrence more reliable.

Useful agreements are possible because not all our interests conflict with those of our opponents. But our mutual
interests are limited, and any realistic agreement is likely
to be a limited one and to contain safeguards against viola-
tion. There is no magic in agreement. In almost every
year from the end of World War I to the start of World
War II, the United States, England and France negotiated
international agreements to limit armaments. But neg-
lected controls and penalties. And their zeal was hardly
diminished by the overt violations of these agreements by
the Japanese, the Germans and the Italians. The chronicle

makes instructive reading today. Only a few months after the Japanese troops in 1931 opened their offensive in Manchuria, 60 nations met in a General Disarmament Conference which, in time, drafted plans to limit warships, abolish submarines and, ultimately, to eliminate military aircraft. On March 7, 1936 Germany reoccupied the Rhineland, violating the Versailles and Locarno Treaties; scarcely two weeks later, a treaty for the limitation of naval arms was signed at London by seven powers. On July 7, 1937 the Japanese invaded China; 10 days later the English concluded bilateral agreements with Germany and the U.S.S.R. And so it went up to the eve of the war. It is not too much to say that, for the Western powers in the interval between World War I and World War II, the international treaties were little more than formal records of their decisions to cut their own national budgets. The treaties were rationalizations for unilateral disarmament.

While it is true that arms have never staved off war indefinitely, the same must be said for arms limitations agreements. An agreement cannot be taken as either good or bad without an examination of its contents. If both sides are wary, the arrangements instituted are likely to be better for both sides than was the status quo before the agreement; and, more important, living up to the agreement will be better than violating it.

It is often claimed that the enormous dangers of the nuclear age should make agreement easier now. They may make agreement more urgent, but in crucial respects it is harder. A wishful and careless plan would be much more dangerous than before the last war. Nuclear weapons offer an enormous advantage to the aggressor. They make retaliation much harder to achieve, thus giving no automatic assurance that an aggressor will be punished. Even a partial disarmament, if one-sided, could invite the debacle. And *total* disarmament, in spite of its rhetorical usefulness, is really understood by both sides to be out of the question in a world of divided sovereignties. In such a world, if one side were totally disarmed the concealment of even a few nuclear weapons by the other side would enable it to dominate. It is a hard truth that for the foreseeable future arms control arrangements can only complement national defenses.

Both sides recognize implicitly that some arms arrangements might worsen the chance of peace. The Russians fear that Western proposals for inspection will furnish the West with intelligence useable in aggression. The West on the other hand fears (correctly) that, in the absence of adequate inspection, the Russians would be free to violate agreements secretly and so obtain the means to dominate. Enthusiasts for agreement suggest, all too easily, that the current arms negotiators in Geneva are mad, or simply lacking in common sense. But the negotiators are not mad or senseless. To devise agreements that reduce rather than increase the possibilities for aggression takes great inventiveness and sober study. A realistic arms control arrangement has to be founded on a mutual interest and a recognition that this mutuality is only partial. The West is quite right in saying that agreements should not be based on faith. If both sides had real faith, no agreement would be necessary. It would be more nearly accurate to say that sound arms control arrangements can be based only on an explicit and precise mutual distrust.

The best reason for any specific arms agreement is to reduce the risk of war. For us the most trivial, almost frivolous, motive for agreement is to reduce a nation's defense budget—that is, the level of effort. But there is no evidence that a mutually useful agreement would permit less effort. Not counting the large cost of an adequate control system, any realistic agreement for reduction in one area is likely to call for increased effort in others. Nuclear disengagement in Europe, for example, might increase the stability of the peace, but it would require the reversal of our NATO military policy and a new emphasis on non-nuclear forces.

On no subject has discussion been more confused and inconsistent than on the above-mentioned level of American effort. On the one hand we are told that Americans are fat, self-indulgent, undisciplined and at the highest peak of material prosperity. On the other, we hear the customary references to the "crushing economic burden of the arms race." As fortresses are invariably "impregnable," risks "calculated" and disarmament "moral," so the burden of the arms race is always "crushing." There have been direful predictions since the end of World War II that an attempt to defend ourselves will turn America into a garrison state. But our defense budget has varied from 40% to 5% to 15% and down again to 9% of our gross national product, and our experience offers little confirmation for such fears. Whether or not Americans and Western Europeans are self-indulgent, they were never richer, and they consume more each year. The U.S. government has estimated that our gross national product will increase from $500 billion to $750 billion in the next decade.

The most important implication of our great prosperity and rate of increase in productive power is that we can afford larger efforts for economic development, for reducing the risks of thermonuclear war and for protecting the political independence and self-development of the non-Communist world. Furthermore we may be able to do it with only a modest sacrifice. In fact, I know of no responsible proposals for meeting these goals that have called for any reduction in our peak level of spending for immediate enjoyment. The widely discussed defense program recommended by the Rockefeller Brothers Fund, for example, could easily be accommodated by the growth in our gross national product predicted by the government—with no decrease in consumer spending but only a temporary slowing in the rate of its growth.

Would the American public make this mild "sacrifice?" That seems to me to depend on what the public thinks the sacrifice is for. Rather too much has been made of the frivolity and self-indulgence of the fat American public. An analysis of consumer expenditures hardly sustains the claim. Consumers have increased their spending for such sober purposes as medical care and education faster than the rise in their incomes and faster than the increase in spending for recreation or for the iniquitous tail fins. None of this seems foolish. In particular there is no reason to believe that Americans would not make a greater effort to accomplish their major purposes if they understood that the risks of *not* making such an effort were large and the rewards for effort were great. But I doubt that the public of this country was ever less informed on matters directly affecting its life and death. On the contrary, at each great crisis the public has been reassured that no further effort is required.

Leaders of opinion have a large responsibility here to inform the public and widen discussion. The great issues of war and peace deserve to be treated candidly and objectively, without wishfulness or hysteria. It is not only the politicians who have been deficient in these respects. In my view, the scientists also have performed poorly. They have been bitterly divided and both extremes have tended to use the authority of science rather than its method—to be wishful and impassioned rather than objective. What is needed is sober thought about the concrete problems of extending democracy inside our own country, of helping the economic and political self-development of other countries and of negotiating without illusion to settle differences with our antagonists while maintaining the military strength to discourage their use of force.

These are tall orders. They cannot be filled quickly, or finally, or by means of some semiautomatic gadget, or in one heroic burst of energy. Nor will the answer come to us in a dream. I suspect that in the wide range of activities we must undertake, dreaming will require the least discipline and the least attention to diet. Our problem is more like that of training for a steep, rocky climb. If, as we are told, America is no longer a youth, we may yet hope to exploit the advantages of maturity: strength, endurance, judgment, responsibility, freedom from the extremes of optimism and pessimism—and steadiness of purpose.

A purpose is not the same thing as a wish. Or a dream. Or even a mission. But one fundamental purpose of a democracy is the exercise of reasoned choice, the conscious shaping of events. Even setbacks would be more meaningful if—to use Hamilton's phrase—instead of being ruled by "accident," we could govern ourselves by "reflection and choice." If the hard problems of our time stir us to more reflective choice, then they will have helped us fulfill one important purpose of a democratic society.

IX

Our History Suggests a Remedy

JAMES RESTON

IF IT IS TRUE THAT AMERICA NEEDS AND LACKS A SENSE OF purpose, the history of the nation suggests a remedy.

For if George Washington had waited for the doubters to develop a sense of purpose in the 18th century, he'd still be crossing the Delaware. In fact, most of the great political crises of the American past have been resolved, not by the zeal and purpose of the people, but usually by the will power or obstinacy of their leaders.

No doubt the massive thirst of a long-tormented majority brought back 3.2 beer, but the plain fact is that in most other emergencies, a resolute minority has usually prevailed over an easy-going or wobbly majority whose primary purpose was to be left alone.

John Adams estimated that one-third of the population was against the American Revolution, one-third for it, and one-third indifferent. And this is the way it has usually been.

Some far-sighted character like Thomas Jefferson or Teddy Roosevelt was always buying Louisiana or the Panama Canal when nobody was looking, and writers have always been grumbling, mainly to each other, about the feebleness of the national will.

The main difference between today's lamentations and those of the past is that the language is milder and the pay better. Thomas Paine, roaring about America's mulish indifference in 1775, makes today's orators sound complacent. And even Ralph Waldo Emerson, who was really a pretty cheery fellow, could wail in 1847:

"Alas for America, the air is loaded with poppy, with imbecility, with dispersion and sloth. . . . Eager, solicitous, hungry, rabid, busy-bodied America: catch thy breath and correct thyself."

Thus, criticism of the American people for lack of purpose is not new. What is new is that leaders now seem to think they must follow the nation instead of leading it. What is new is that a hostile coalition of nations now has the military power to destroy the Republic. The margin of error granted to us in past wars and crises has vanished. What could be won before with partial effort, late starts, feeble alliances and mediocre administration can no longer be won in a contest with the Communists.

It is not that they are so efficient but that they are so purposeful. They are all working on the main target and we are not. Life, tyranny and the pursuit of Capitalists is the Russian way of life. They have obliterated the difference between war and peace. They are always at war, all of them, women as well as men—teachers, philosophers, scientists, engineers, lady discus throwers, airmen, and three or four million foot soldiers.

None of this need trouble us very much except for *their* national purpose, which is simply to replace our system of individual freedom with their system of state control wherever they can, including regions vital to our security such as Germany, Japan and even Cuba.

I must say they have been very frank about it. They have given us timely if not fair warning. They are directing all the energies of all their people to that goal. They are not arguing about the conflict between private interests and the national interest. They have simply eliminated private interest. They have put everybody to work on "burying" capitalism, and since our national purpose, among other things, is to avoid being buried, this creates an awkward and even nasty situation.

How, then, shall we approach the problem? I was brought up on the Church of Scotland's shorter catechism, the first question of which is: "What is the chief end of man?"

Accordingly, I am all for self-direction and self-criticism. Nevertheless, I have my doubts about the imminence of any self-induced renaissance or epoch of austerity.

When I consider attacking the problem through the people, I think of Harry Ashmore's old story about the man who acquired a reputation for training mules with honeyed words and kindness. Hearing about this remarkable achievement, the Society for the Prevention of Cruelty to Animals dispatched a lady emissary to present the mule-trainer with a medal.

Upon arrival, she asked for a demonstration. The trainer obligingly trotted out a young mule, reached for a long two-by-four, and clouted the beast over the head. As the mule struggled back to his feet the good lady exclaimed in horror, "Good heavens, man, I thought you trained these animals with kindness."

"I do, ma'am," he replied, "but first I got to git the critters' attention."

I don't know how just anybody gets the attention of 180 million people these days. They are engaged in the pursuit of happiness, which, incidentally, the Declaration of Independence spells with a capital "H," and to be frank about it, I suspect that public debates on the national purpose give them a pain.

It will not, I think, be wise to underestimate America's current resistance to exhortations from the preachers, professors, columnists and editorial writers of the nation. For unless I miss my guess, the Americano, *circa* 1960, is in no mood to rush off on his own initiative to "emancipate the human race," or to set any new records as the greatest benefactor of all time, or engage in any of the other crusades mapped out for him in Cambridge, Mass.

He may do many of these things because he is honest enough to know that he doesn't know all the facts of this dangerous and complicated era, but he is not likely to set out to do them because of his own "reflection and reason" or the arguments of talkers or writers he seldom sees.

Accordingly, we must, I think start with the national leadership, partly because this is the engine that has pulled us out of the mud before, and partly because this is an election year, when we will be picking a President, probably for most of the nineteen sixties.

The president of the United States is the one man who can get the attention of the American people. If he says the nation is in trouble, they will listen to him. If he addresses himself to their doubts and questions, they will hear him out. If he presents programs and legislation to do what he thinks is necessary for the safety of the Republic and explains and keeps explaining why these are essential, he may very well prevail.

All the magazine articles on the national purpose, all the reports by all the foundations on all our manifold weaknesses, all the speeches by Adlai Stevenson, Jack Kennedy, Lyndon Johnson and Stuart Symington on the wickedness of the Republicans, all the exhortations to return to the faith of our fathers—all are nothing compared to serious programs eloquently expressed and strongly pushed by a determined president of the United States.

"His is the only national voice in affairs," wrote Woodrow Wilson. "Let him once win the admiration and confidence of the country and no other single force can withstand him, no combination of forces will easily overpower him. His position takes the imagination of the country. . . . His is the vital place of action in the system. . . ."

Of course, he has to act. He cannot ask for half-measures and run away. But once he expresses the national need, once he decides to try to remove rather than to perpetuate the illusions of the past, then his specific remedies will affect the spirit and direction of the nation.

I remember when the Marshall Plan for Europe was devised in Washington. It was perfectly obvious that the sickness of the European economy was creating a crisis of great magnitude, and the bare bones of a four-year plan, costing perhaps as much as $20,000,000,000, were worked out and approved by President Truman.

I printed a long story about it one Sunday in the New York *Times,* and by 10 o'clock that morning, the late Senator Arthur H. Vandenberg of Michigan, then Chairman of the Foreign Relations Committee, called me at home and said: "You must be out of your senses. No administration would dare to come to the Senate with a proposal like that."

Yet once the lead was taken and the need documented, Senator Vandenberg ended up as a key supporter of what almost everybody agrees was the most far-sighted piece of legislation since the war.

I do not underestimate the task. I agree with much that has been said in these essays about the slackness of our society, but I find the present mood understandable, perhaps inevitable, under the circumstances, and not without hope.

At the end of the last war, the American people made a genuine effort to clear the wreckage and understand the new situation. They went through the biggest geography and history lesson in their history, always with the false optimism that they were dealing with a temporary situation that would eventually go away.

Instead of going away, the problems became larger and more complex: after Europe, it was the Middle East; after the Middle East, the Far East; after the Far East, Africa; after Africa, outer space; and after outer space a lot of inner tensions over U-2, me too, inflation, deflation, rising cost of living, balance of payments, nuclear testing, sputniks, luniks and a lot of other things that everybody seemed to be differing about.

There was no panic about any of this. The people merely turned from what they did not understand to what they did understand. They turned inward from the world to the community and the family. In the 15 years of the atomic age, they increased the population of the nation by more than 40,000,000, which is not the action of a frightened people, and which is interesting when you think that the entire population of the country at the start of the Civil War 100 years ago was only 31,000,000.

A distinction has to be made, I think, between the façade of America and the other more genuine America. There is, of course, this big obvious clattering America of Hollywood and Madison Avenue and Washington, but there is also the outer, quieter America, which has either kept its religious faith or at least held on to the morality derived from religious tradition.

I do not wish to glorify the multitude. Much can be said about the dubious effects on the American character of very early marriage, easy credit, cheap booze, cheaper TV, low education standards, and job security even for sloppy work.

Nevertheless, there is more concern for the outside world, more interest in its problems, more generosity, and more resourcefulness in this society than in any free society I know anything about.

If it is true, as I believe, that this generation of Americans is doing less than it could, it is also true that it has done everything it was asked to do. It may be more concerned about its private interests than about the public interest, but if a man is offered a choice between a Cadillac and swift kick in the pants, we should not be surprised if he doesn't bend over.

What has it been asked to do that it has not done?

It was asked to restore the broken economy of Europe, and it helped bring that continent, within a decade, to the highest level of prosperity in history.

It was asked to accept high taxation and military conscription to police the world, and it has done so from the North Cape of Norway to Japan and Korea.

It was asked to keep a standing army of a quarter of a million men in Western Europe and it has done so for 15 years, with scarcely a murmur of protest from a single American politician.

It was asked to abandon its tradition of isolation, and it took on more responsibilities involving more risks—in Korea and elsewhere—than the British ever did at the height of their imperial power.

These are not the acts of a slack and decadent people. There is nothing in the record of free peoples to compare with it. This is not a static society. The problem is merely that the pace of history has outrun the pace of change. Ideas and policies have lagged behind events, so that by the time policies were formulated, debated, and put in force, the situations they were intended to remedy had changed.

Thus, in a torrent of change, in a revolution of science, a social revolution at home and an unprecedented political revolution in Asia, Africa, and Latin America, it is scarcely surprising that there is a crisis of understanding in the nation. This is all the more true because there has been a serious weakening of the ties between the men of ideas and the men of politics in this country during the last decade.

"Our slow world," wrote Woodrow Wilson in 1890, "spends its time catching up with the ideas of its best minds. It would seem that in almost every generation men are born who embody the projected consciousness of their time and people.

"Their thought runs forward apace into the regions whither the race is advancing, but where it will not for many a weary day arrive. . . . The new thoughts of one age are the commonplaces of the next.

"The men who act stand nearer to the mass than the men who write; and it is in their hands that new thought gets its translation into the crude language of deeds . . ."

It cannot be said that the men of ideas in the country have not performed in these last few years their traditional tasks. They have observed the convulsions of our time and let their minds run ahead to the logical consequences for the nation.

I cannot remember a time when there has been more purposeful thought on contemporary problems in the universities and foundations than now. Their reports and conclusions would fill a good-sized library, but the alliance between them and the White House has been feeble, and somehow it must be restored.

What, then, can be done?

We can, at least, look at the world as it is instead of the world as we would like it to be. In the 43 years since the Soviet revolution—of which 25 have been devoted to establishing their regime and fighting the last world war—they have brought their industrial production to about 45% of ours.

Since the war, their rate of growth has been between 9 and 10% while ours has been in the neighborhood of 3%. They are having trouble with their agricultural production, but if they and we both continue at the present rates of growth, the experts figure they will have approximately as much effective industrial production as the United States in 1975.

On the face of it, this may not worry the American people, but it is perfectly obvious that the trend is running against us in this field, and that, as former Secretary of State Dean Acheson says, the likelihood is that Moscow will do three things with this new production: 1. Increase their military capabilities. 2. Increase their resources for economic penetration in the underdeveloped nations, and 3. By a combination of these two, demonstrate to the uncommitted countries of the world that the Soviet Union is the country of spectacular growth, and that the Communist system is the way to lift new countries in a short time into the new scientific age.

It is this latter point, rather than the threat of nuclear war against the United States, that concerns most students of the problem.

The Russians have already increased their exports to underdeveloped countries to about $3 million. They have five thousand people administering these programs. And they are directing them primarily in six countries of considerable political importance to the U.S.S.R.

It is much harder to understand the threat of this kind of economic penetration than it is to understand the threat of indirect Communist aggression, as, for example, in Korea. But the threat is there just the same.

Since the last war, 1.2 billion people have changed their form of government in the world, and 800 million of these have achieved independence for the first time. These new nations are determined to be industrialized, ready or not. Hunger and pestilence are not new in the world, but the 2 billion hungry people are less willing to tolerate hunger and pestilence now that they know something can be done about it.

How these new governments develop, in freedom or by the quicker way of state control, may very well determine, not only the climate of freedom in the world, but the balance of power as well.

Thus the primary problem of foreign affairs may very well be, not the East-West problem we hear so much about, but what Sir Oliver Frank calls the North-South problem: whether the nations of the South, in Africa, Asia, and Latin America, develop along the lines of the free industrialized nations of the north, or the state-controlled methods of the two large Communist northern states of the Soviet Union and China.

We have tended to make several assumptions about this: that most nations wanted to develop like the United States, that knowledge cannot develop except in a climate of freedom, and that the Western powers could deal with the underdeveloped nations without interfering much with present concepts of sovereignty or commercial practice.

All these assumptions are now under challenge. The Soviet Union has shown that spectacular scientific progress can be made in a closed society. Cuba, to take only one example close at hand, has not only indicated contempt for the American system of free enterprise but is now organizing its whole society under state control.

The problem is not that the Soviet Union produces better engineers than the United States—though it certainly produces more—but that it can direct its engineers into these new countries or anywhere else that helps promote the purpose of the state.

As Dean McGeorge Bundy of Harvard has pointed out: "It may be that we are at the edge of a time in which authoritarian societies, controlling and using this new investment, the human mind, will be able to produce revolutions in power and in growth as remarkable to us as our own revolution, the industrial and technological revolution of the last 150 years, is remarkable today to the people who inhabit the world of rising expectations.

"To me, this hazardous possibility that centralized control of technology and of science behind it may lead to a new order of growth, of power, and of change in the hands of people with a high degree of political purpose and centralized and ruthless control . . . seems to be the real danger in the growth of Soviet and Chinese power."

My conclusions about all this mysterious sociology and economics are unoriginal, vague, and even modest. All I know about the "rate of growth" is what happened to three boys of my own in the last 23 years, and even that is a little confusing. It would be pleasant to think, however, that all this concern in the nation among serious men about the higher rate of growth in the U.S.S.R. was seriously discussed and not dismissed as another left-wing trick to increase the size of government or elect some Democrat.

First, therefore, an honest debate on the issue might not be a bad idea. Maybe we cannot do everything everywhere. Maybe after 125 years of isolation and a generation of internationalism, somebody should call out once more to America: "Catch thy breath and correct thyself."

But anyway, a revival of honest plain talk in the country wouldn't do any harm.

Second, in the face of the clear facts, anything less than the highest possible standard of education for the children of America is obviously a disgrace. We cannot punch kids out like cookies and drop them into slots, and wouldn't if we could; but we ought to be able to spend more money on their education than we do on all that sexy advertising.

Third, offhand, I would guess we were kidding ourselves

in thinking we could do this job with the kind of people now working on it overseas or that we could do it without far more cooperation and coordination among the allies.

If the main war now is the battle in the underdeveloped areas, why not offer talented young men of draft age the option of using their brains in a civilian service in Indochina rather than sentencing them to Army KP in Hoboken?

It is not fair or accurate to say that the voluntary system cannot compete with the directed system in recruiting men for service in the underdeveloped areas, for no really imaginative effort has been made to attract the volunteers.

Thus, wherever you look it is hard to escape the conclusion that our response is unequal to the threat. We are in what Professor Walt Whitman Rostow of the Massachusetts Institute of Technology calls one of those "neurotic fixations of history." These are periods when nations are confronted by radically new situations but hang on to old policies that are increasingly divorced from reality.

This is what George III of England did when confronted by what he called the "rebellion" of the American colonies, what Edward VIII did when he hung on to Wally Simpson, what Stanley Baldwin did when he refused to rearm Britain in the face of Hitler's challenge and what the United States did when it clung to isolation after the rise of Nazi Germany.

Isolation is now gone, but the hangover of the old habits of the days of isolation remain; in our assumptions that we can meet the Soviet challenge with the same school system, the same political patronage system, the same diplomatic system, the same attitudes toward politics and the public service, and the same old chestnut about private interests inevitably serving the public interest.

It is not so much that we have lost our way forward but that we have lost our way home. This is the country of freedom, youth, experimentation, and innovation; of pioneers and missionaries and adventures.

If you ask whether we can meet the Soviet challenge by concentrating on our private interests instead of on the public interest, by losing a great many of our best young brains in poor schools before they ever get to the college level, by not using our intelligent women when the Russians are using theirs, by not making a genuine effort to get our best brains into the most effective jobs to serve the nation, why I'm bound to say that the answer is "no."

I believe, however, that there is still a lot of spunk and spirit in this country that can be brought by free methods into the service of the nation, provided presidential power is used to clarify where the nation stands.

The first national purpose is to know who we are and what we stand for; it would be an impertinence to try to improve on the second paragraph of the Declaration of Independence as a guide to the problem.

"We hold these truths to be self-evident," it says in the first sentence. It thereupon lists, as if they were the indisputable facts of last Sunday's American League batting averages, a whole catalogue of wonderful things that are not only not "self-evident" in 1960, but are actually in violent dispute among men all over the world, including quite a few in our own country.

"All men are created equal," it says, and, of course, this is just the trouble, for you can get an argument on that one anywhere in the province of Georgia, U.S.S.R., or the state of Georgia, U.S.A.

In the minds of the Founding Fathers, the moral idea came before the political, and the latter was merely an expression of the former. This, too, was apparently the idea Matthew Arnold had in mind when he came to this country before the turn of the century and discussed our national purpose in New York.

He made two points:

"We must hold fast to the austere but true doctrine," he said, "as to what really governs politics, overrides with an inexorable fatality the combinations of so-called politicians, and saves or destroys states.

"Having in mind things true, things elevated, things just, things pure, things amiable, things of good report: having these in mind, studying and loving these, is what saves states."

However, the old gentleman, when writing these exuberant sentences had no illusion about their being put into force by the majority. These moral concepts would prevail, he said, only as they were upheld by "the remnant" of leaders and thinkers who loved wisdom, for the majority, he insisted, was full of "prosperities, idolatries, oppression, luxury, pleasures and careless women. . . . That shall come to nought and pass away."

"The remnant" in America of those who love wisdom and have the ability to compete with any nation in the world is very large. It has greatly increased as the population of the nation has increased, but it needs to be brought to bear on the great purposes of the nation more than it is today, and this is obviously one task of presidential leadership.

Meanwhile, there is no cause to despair over the evidence of disorder and menace, for in all the golden ages of history, disorder and hazard have existed alongside vitality and creativeness.

"Surely our age shares many characteristics with the earlier golden times," Caryl P. Haskins, President of the Carnegie Institution of Washington, has written. "Theirs is the wide feeling of insecurity, the deep-lying anxiety, the sense of confusion, not unlike the earlier times in general character . . .

"But there is likewise the same intense concern with new ideas and new concepts, the same eagerness for widened vistas of understanding . . ."

What Mr. Haskins did not say was that these golden ages were also periods of great leaders who knew how to bring ideas and politics together, and this seems to me to be the heart of our present problem.

X

National Purpose

WALTER LIPPMANN

IN A RATHER SPECIAL SENSE AMERICANS HAVE ALWAYS BEEN a purposeful nation. For the country is settled by the descendants of people who pulled up their roots in the old societies, and crossed the wide ocean for a purpose. Always they came with a sense that they would make for themselves a better life in a new world. They believed that they had new work to do and that all who saw their example would be enlightened and inspired by it.

The bond of American union has not been piety and reverence for the past but a conviction of purpose and of the destiny it would bring for posterity. America has always been not only a country but a dream. There has always been a general and unquestioned belief that here on this soil there would be demonstrated to mankind the blessings of freedom: as the shackles and servitudes of the past were put away, there would arise a great and glorious society.

And so, until very recently at least, we have looked upon it as in the nature of things that for America nothing is finished, that this is a young nation still in the beginnings of its career in the world. From this sense of purpose and of the American destiny we have drawn energy and confidence. Americans have been a nation of exuberant optimists, sniffing the air with a buoyant feeling that it is the early morning and that it is good to be alive. Evil and the perversities of fate and the burdens of mortality were not more than obstacles to be gotten at and overcome.

There were no insoluble human problems. At the worst, there were problems that it might take a generation or two to master. It never occurred to Americans to ask whether they were going to "survive." They had just begun to live. Nor did they worry about the consequences of becoming rich, fat, lazy, self-indulgent, self-centered and beset with the illusion that the present can be made to last forever. For they were not yet rich and they had to work hard for a living.

*   *   *

If, as so many of us think today, we are now without such a general and inspired sense of national purpose, where shall we look for the cause and the remedy?

The cause of the vacancy is, I believe, this: we have reached a point in our internal development and in our relations with the rest of the world where we have fulfilled and outlived most of what we used to regard as the program of our national purposes.

We are rather like a man whose purpose it is to cross the continent, and having started from New York he has gotten to Chicago. Which way shall he go then? There is more than one way to cross the continent, and until he has chosen which way and then has worked out the intermediate stops, he will remain in Chicago, feeling worried and without a sense of direction and of clear purpose.

As I see it, the American people today are like the man who got to Chicago, and needs a new road map to show him the way from there on.

In this century, the sense of national purpose has been a composite wrought under three innovating Presidents, under Theodore Roosevelt, Woodrow Wilson and Franklin Roosevelt. They led the country on the road which it has taken for some 50 years—since America emerged as a great power in the world, and since here at home it has become an ever more industrialized and urbanized society.

Time has passed and history has not stood still. The Roosevelt-Wilson-Roosevelt formulae and policies and programs no longer fit the character of the world Americans are now concerned with, the world as it has developed since the second World War. We are now waiting to be shown the way into the future. We are waiting for another innovator in the line of the two Roosevelts and Wilson.

The innovator for whom the country is waiting will not come with a new revelation of the ultimate ends and commitments of our society. The ultimate ends are fixed. They are lasting and they are not disputed. The nation is dedicated to freedom. It is dedicated to the rights of man and to government with the consent of the governed. The innovation, which is now beginning, will be in the means, in the policies and programs and measures, by which the ultimate ends of our free society can be realized in the world today.

My thesis is that to affirm the ultimate ends—as every public man does in almost every speech—is not a substitute for, is not the equivalent of declaring our national purpose and of leading the nation. These affirmations are like standing up when the *Star-Spangled Banner* is played, and then doing nothing further about anything. They beg the question, which is not whither the nation should go, but how it should get there.

The remedy, then, will not be found in the restatement of our ideals, however resounding the rhetoric. It will be found in the innovation of the political formulae, the concrete measures, the practical programs, by which our ideals can be realized in the greatly changed world we now live in. I feel sure that innovators will appear with the new generation that is rising to power. For it is not the nation which is old, but only its leaders.

Broadly speaking, there have been two great epochs in our history, each with its own dominant national purpose. The first epoch extended from the middle of the 18th Century down through the 19th. Beginning with the colonial wars of the 18th Century and then with the founding of the Republic, the central national purpose of the American people was to open up the continental territory, to consolidate that territory firmly within the American union and to make the territory invulnerably secure as against all other powers.

In the pursuit of this national purpose, the American colonists fought the French and the Indians. The independent American nation fought the British and the Spanish and the Mexicans and the Indians. It fought a great and terrible Civil War to preserve the union of its territory. Officially, it may be said that this epoch, during which the national purpose was to consolidate the national territory, ended in 1890 when the last of our 37 wars with the Indians was concluded.

After the turn of the century, the original national American purpose having been fulfilled, a new epoch began. It began, we may say, with Theodore Roosevelt's recognition that the United States was no longer a sheltered and semidependent nation but that, having settled the continental territory, it had become one of the great powers. Theodore Roosevelt, who was a far-seeing innovator, saw too that the United States was no longer a rural nation of independent farmers. Increasingly, it was becoming an industrial society inhabited by great corporations which exercised powers that often challenged the authority of the established government itself.

The innovation begun by Theodore Roosevelt was carried further by Woodrow Wilson. Wilson accepted reluctantly the burden of our being a great power. When he was forced into the first World War, he attempted to define a national purpose which would reduce the burden of being a great power. He began by declaring that the world must be made safe for democracy and ended by demanding that it become democratic.

This has proved to be an aspiration rather than a purpose and a policy and a program. For had it become a national purpose, the nation would have found itself committed to a perpetual crusade and, therefore, to perpetual war. Nevertheless, the aspiration, though it is quite unrealizable in a very great part of the world, has become an element of the American conscience. Even when we feel compelled to subsidize some of our more primitive clients, the Wilsonian ideology makes us uneasy and embarrassed.

When Franklin Roosevelt became President, he found himself, rather unexpectedly, confronted with the breakdown of the established economic order. Contrary also to his hope and to his expectations, he was confronted with the rise of a new thing in modern history—the monster of the totalitarian state. Necessity became the mother of invention. It demanded the improvisation of a new national purpose in domestic and in foreign affairs. The innovations of Roosevelt were a grand improvisation.

From the New Deal, particularly from the second phase of it when Roosevelt turned from a planned economy to a compensated economy, the present generation of Americans have inherited the formulae of their political actions. They have inherited the compensated economy and the welfare state, and no serious person in either party would now propose to repeal and undo them.

In foreign affairs, the country learned in the second World War that it was no longer one among many great powers but that in fact it was the leading power upon which the whole Western world depended for its security and for leadership. This is a burden and a responsibility and a danger and a demand upon our resources and a test of our wisdom which the first Roosevelt and Wilson never anticipated, which the second Roosevelt began to be aware of from about the middle of the war to the time of his death.

In the 15 years which have passed since the end of the second World War, the condition of mankind has changed more rapidly and more deeply than in any other period within the experience of the American people. There has been a swift and radical change in the balance of power in the world. Among the masses of the people in the underdeveloped countries there is in all the continents a mounting revolution. There is a radical change in the technology of war and in the technology of industry. There is in the United States and in the advanced countries a great and threatening agglomeration of peoples in cities. There is a menacing increase in the population of the world. There is a development of the mass media of communication which, because it marks a revolution in popular education and in the presentation of information, and in the very nature of debate and deliberation, is affecting profoundly the assumptions of the older democratic system.

Nobody, it is fair to say, not the most sensitive and knowing among us, is as yet able to realize fully what all these changes mean and to point out specifically and with sufficient clarity how this country should deal with them. But what we do know is that the formulations of national purpose which were made in the first half of this century are now inadequate. In part we have fulfilled them. In part we have outlived them. In part they have become irrelevant because of the unexpected changes in the condition of things. In part they are out of focus. All in all, they do not now mobilize our energies.

Necessity will again be the mother of invention, and in the time to come we shall close the gap which now exists between the new realities and the old formulations of our national purpose. I do not presume to anticipate the innovators for whom we are waiting. But there is already visible, it seems to me, the shape of the land across which the innovators must lead the nation.

Thus, for the first time in American experience we are confronted with a rival power which denies the theory and the practice of our society, and has forced upon us a competition for the leadership of the world. This challenge coincides with the radically new fact that the oceans have ceased to be our ramparts and that our land is no longer invulnerable.

As there is no chance that our immensely formidable rival will disarm or disappear, we shall have to live in the same world with him. We shall have to solve problems which did not exist for Wilson and for the two Roosevelts. We shall have to devise ways of protecting our vital interests, which are world-wide, and we shall have to do this without precipitating an insoluble crisis that would generate an inevitable war. This will demand a deep reformulation of our foreign policy, which has hitherto been, and in a great part still is, addressed to a very different world situation. It will demand a re-education of American opinion, not only when it yearns for the lost innocence of our old isolation but also when it plunges into a new globalism which supposes that we are omnipotent, and averts its eyes from the hard reality of the power of the Communist bloc.

We know, of course, that the challenge is a broad one. The competition is in the whole field of national power. It is a competition not only in military power but in all forms of power, the power to produce wealth and the power to use wealth for education, for the advancement of science and for public as well as private ends.

On our success in achieving military security by arms and by an astute diplomacy depend our national existence. Our ability to meet the whole challenge depends upon our success in learning to use our growing wealth for something more than more and more private satisfaction. It depends upon our being able and willing to use it for

imponderable and immaterial ends, like science and education and the public amenities.

To use increments of our growing wealth wisely and
prudently for public and immaterial ends: that is the goal,
so I believe, toward which our national purpose will now
be directed. We have to pay for defense, and there can
be no serious dispute that we must pay for it. But we have
also to be able and willing to pay for the things which
cannot be consumed privately, such as the education of
children, the development of beautiful cities, and the advancement of knowledge. We have to be able and willing
to pay for what is, to put it briefly, civilization itself.

At bottom, we have to do these things because they need
to be done, because they have to be done, and because they
are supremely worth doing. Even if we were not challenged, we would need to do them for their own sake. We
would need to do them even if the Soviet Union and the
whole Communist orbit were still where they were 50 years
ago.

But now we are in fact challenged, and because of that
we must do these civilized things, not only to make a better
life for ourselves but in order to mobilize the power to
avoid a much worse life. Were there no great rival and
challenger, we might dawdle along, we might indulge in
a growing private affluence while we suffered a declining
national greatness. But for us there is no choice but to
respond to the challenge, even though this demands that
we change many of our cherished dogmas and harden ourselves to a sterner way of life. For our freedom and our
system of democratic government are not likely to survive just because we believe in them and enjoy them. We
shall have to prove that with them and through them we

can satisfy the needs of our people and be equal to the challenge of the time we live in.

Western freedom will not survive just because it is a noble ideal. In the age we live in it will survive if, and I think only if, we can take freedom down with us into the hurly-burly of the competition and conflict and prove that a free society can make itself the good society.

I should like to add a postscript to express a personal feeling about the challenge we face and the response we must make. It is that with all the danger and trouble and worry it causes us, the Soviet challenge may yet prove to have been a blessing in disguise. For without it, what would become of us if we felt that we were invulnerable, if our influence in the world were undisputed, if we had no need to prove that we can rise above a comfortable, tranquil, self-satisfaction?

We would, I feel sure, slowly deteriorate and fall apart, having lost our great energies because we did not exercise them, having lost our daring because everything was so warm and so comfortable and so cozy. We would then have entered into the decline which has marked the closing period in the history of so many societies—when they have gotten everything they wanted, when they have come to think that there is no great work to be done, and that the purpose of life is to hold on and stay put. For then the night has come and they doze off and they begin to die.

APPENDIX

I

JOHN K. JESSUP is chief editorial writer of *Life* magazine.

He was born in Rochester, New York, in 1907. He was graduated from Yale University in 1928, taught English there, and served as assistant editor of the *Yale Alumni Weekly*. He was an advertising copywriter until he joined Time, Inc., in 1935, as a writer for *Fortune* magazine.

In 1940 he was transferred to *Time* magazine. When Time, Inc., formed a committee in 1942 to study the postwar outlook, Mr. Jessup was named its chairman. He was responsible for the preparation of reports published periodically during World War II as a supplement to *Fortune*.

He became chief editorial writer for *Life* in 1944. From 1948 to 1951 he served in other capacities for Time, Inc., then returned to *Life* as chief editorial writer.

II

ADLAI EWING STEVENSON, Democrat, was twice a candidate for the presidency, opposing Dwight D. Eisenhower, Republican.

Mr. Stevenson was born in Los Angeles in 1900. He received his Bachelor's degree from Princeton in 1922 and his Law degree from Northwestern University in 1926.

After practicing law in Chicago, he was assistant to the Secretary of the Navy from 1941 to 1944, assistant to the Secretary of State in 1945, and United States delegate to the United Nations General Assembly in 1946 and 1947.

He served as Governor of Illinois from 1949 to 1953.

Mr. Stevenson is now practicing law in Chicago. He is trustee or director of various educational and philanthropic organizations. He is the author of *Call to Greatness,* published in 1954, and *What I Think,* 1956.

III

ARCHIBALD MacLEISH, poet, won the Bollingen Prize for Poetry in 1953 and Pulitzer Prizes in 1932, 1953 and 1959.

His works include *The Pot of Earth,* published in 1925; *Frescoes for Mr. Rockefeller's City,* 1933; *Collected Poems 1917-1952; Union Pacific—a Ballet,* 1934; *Land of the Free,* 1938; *America Was Promises,* 1939; *Freedom Is the Right to Choose,* 1951, and *J. B.,* 1957.

Mr. MacLeish was born in Glencoe, Illinois, in 1892. He received an A.B. degree at Yale in 1915, an LL.B. at Harvard in 1919 and a Litt.D. from Yale in 1939.

He was Librarian of Congress from 1939 to 1944 and Assistant Secretary of State in 1944-45. He was chairman of the American delegation to the first general conference of the United Nations Educational, Scientific and Cultural Organization at Paris in 1946.

IV

D AVID SARNOFF, board chairman of the Radio Corporation of America, was born in Russia in 1891.

He came to this country in 1900 and six years later started work as an office boy for the Marconi Wireless Telegraph Company. In 1909 he became manager of the Marconi station at Sea Gate, Brooklyn, and later served as a wireless operator for the Marconi company.

Mr. Sarnoff became commercial manager for R.C.A. when it absorbed Marconi in 1919. He became general manager and vice-president of R.C.A. in 1922.

Meantime he had studied electrical engineering at Pratt Institute in Brooklyn. He received the degree of Doctor of Science from St. Lawrence University in 1927. He has been R.C.A. chairman since 1947.

Mr. Sarnoff served in the Army and was made a brigadier general in the Reserve in 1944.

V

WILLIAM FRANKLIN GRAHAM is the evangelist and Baptist minister better known as Billy Graham.

He was born in Charlotte, North Carolina, in 1918. He received a Bachelor of Arts degree from Wheaton College in 1943, a Bachelor of Theology from the Florida Bible Seminary in 1940 and a Doctor of Divinity from Kings College in 1948.

Dr. Graham was president of a small interdenominational school in Minneapolis from 1947 to 1951. He has conducted nationwide campaigns since 1946 and has made seven trips to Europe since World War II.

He is the author of *Calling Youth to Christ,* published in 1947; *Revival in Our Times,* 1950; *America's Hour of Decision,* 1951; *Korean Diary,* 1953 and *Peace With God,* 1953.

He has also written a daily newspaper column, produced religious films, and appeared on radio and television.

VI

JOHN WILLIAM GARDNER, foundation executive, taught psychology before entering foundation work.

He has been president of the Carnegie Corporation of New York and the Carnegie Foundation for the Advancement of Teaching since 1955.

He was born in Los Angeles in 1912. He received an A.B. degree in 1935 and an A.M. in 1936 from Stanford University, and a Ph.D. from the University of California in 1938. From 1936 to 1942 he taught psychology at California, Connecticut College and Mount Holyoke College.

Mr. Gardner served with the Federal Communications Commission in Washington in 1942 and 1943. He was in the Marine Corps from 1943 to 1946.

He became a staff member of the Carnegie Corporation of New York in 1946.

VII

CLINTON LAWRENCE ROSSITER 3D, educator and author, is a widely recognized authority on political science and government.

He has been Professor of Government and chairman of the Department of Government at Cornell University since 1956. Among his books are *Constitutional Dictatorship,* published in 1948; *The Supreme Court and the Commander in Chief,* 1951; *Seedtime of the Republic,* 1953; *Conservatism in America,* 1955; *The First American Presidency,* 1956.

Professor Rossiter was born in Philadelphia in 1917. He received an A.B. from Cornell in 1939; an M.A. from Princeton in 1941, and a Ph.D. from Princeton in 1942.

He served as a Navy lieutenant in World War II, taught political science at Cornell from 1946 to 1954 and was a Guggenheim fellow in 1953-54.

VIII

ALBERT WOHLSTETTER, forty-six, is associate director of projects at the Rand Corporation.

Since 1951 he has conducted studies for the Rand Corporation on the problem of deterring general war and the vulnerability of retaliatory forces. From 1956 to 1959 he was chairman of the strategic air power group of the Rand Corporation, dealing with problems of both offense and defense.

He was scientific adviser to the United States delegation at Geneva during the 1958 discussions with the Russians on the prevention of surprise attack. He has also been a consultant to the State Department.

Mr. Wohlstetter was educated in the New York public schools and Columbia University. In World War II he was a research associate at the National Bureau of Economic Research, a consultant to the War Production Board and an official of Atlas Aircraft Products.

IX

JAMES RESTON was born in Clydebank, Scotland, in 1909.

His parents brought him to the United States the following year, but he returned to Scotland for some of his early schooling and then came back to this country in 1920. He attended public schools in Dayton, Ohio, and graduated from the University of Illinois in 1932.

After holding a number of news and publicity jobs in the Middle West, he joined The Associated Press in 1934 as a sports writer in New York. Three years later the agency sent him to London where he covered the diplomatic activity preceding the outbreak of World War II. In 1939 he joined the London Bureau of the New York *Times* and spent most of the war years in London and Washington. He became the Washington correspondent of the *Times* in 1953.

Mr. Reston won the Pulitzer Prize for his news dispatches in 1944 and 1956. He now writes an editorial page column three times a week in addition to his news reporting.

X

Walter Lippmann, special writer for the New York
Herald Tribune, is known not only as an editor
and journalist, but as a thoughtful critic of American
life.

Born in New York City in 1889, Mr. Lippmann
graduated from Harvard University in 1910. After a
period of free-lancing, he joined the *New Republic,*
when it was founded in 1914; and then went to the
New York *World,* becoming its editor in 1929.

He was assistant to the Secretary of War, 1917; acted
as Colonel E. M. House's secretary in preparing data
for the Paris Peace Conference; and was a captain in
U.S. Army Military Intelligence during the war.

Mr. Lippmann is the author of many books, includ-
ing *The Communist World and Ours, The Public
Philosophy, Isolation and Alliances,* and *The Cold
War.* He is a regular contributor to many magazines.